Bethany L. Connor

D1522789

cherished

*One Woman's Journey
to Love and Be Loved*

Cherished — One Woman's Journey to Love and Be Loved
Copyright 2013 Bethany L. Connor
All rights reserved
Printed in the United States of America

ISBN: 978-1939268-273

Published by Next Century Publishing
www.nextcenturypublishing.com

HOW TO REACH THE AUTHOR:
www.acherishedwoman.com

What Others Are Saying

"This poignant and beautiful story is the struggle of Bethany finding her true self and listening to that voice within. With God in control, Bethany trusts Him and steps into her greatness that's always been inside her. This compelling and heartfelt story is inspiring and a must read."

~ Tom Haupt, International Speaker and Best-Selling Author of *Time-Out! Winning Strategies for Playing a Bigger Game in Life*, www.tomhaupt.com

"*Cherished* is a raw, real and honest look at what drives human behavior and the stories we create around events that happen in our lives. Bethany courageously and vulnerably shares her journey and how she moved from the depths of despair to overflowing joy! Her path is one that we can all follow when we choose to walk the journey. Asking ourselves quality questions will slowly, but surely, unlock the answers to our dreams."

~ Ruby Muza, www.rubymuza.com

"Everyone wants three things in life: to feel valuable, to be heard and to know they made a difference. We like for people to believe we have our act together while we are struggling on the inside. Bethany's book reveals the only plan to relieve the inner pain and live out your divine destiny!"

~ Tim Davis, www.TimDavisOnline.com

"True connection comes through sharing our stories and that's exactly what Bethany does in this book! She opens up her heart in such a compelling way that when you read her story, it's as if you are walking right beside her and experiencing exactly what she is experiencing. It's not an exaggeration to say that this book can transform the way you lead, love, and live!"

~ Kent Julian, www.liveitforward.com

"Vulnerability is what describes Bethany's writings. She puts herself out there — her journey, her pain and her healing not to glamorize the process she went through, but to share her story of finding true love in the One who created her. This book is for anyone who desires to go on a journey to hearing God's voice in their life. Bethany's example will prompt your heart to want more out of this life and more from your relationship with God."

~ Michelle Howe, Leadership Coach with Everyday Lifeline and author of *Copying is the Highest Form of Compliment, Giving Others Permission to Follow Your Lead*, www.iwokeupyesterday.com

"I have had the opportunity to work with Bethany Connor in several life changing seminars. I find that she is a woman of impeccable integrity and insight. Her ability to communicate with clarity and honesty touches everyone with whom she connects both professionally and personally. I suggest that if you are looking for more love in your life or want to have more powerful and secure relationships that you read this book."

~ Patrick Dean, www.seminarsystems.com

"Bethany Connor's *Cherished: One Woman's Journey to Love and Be Loved* captures the human condition of one's limiting beliefs that we all, at some level, hold that we are not 'worthy' or 'good enough.' She takes us on her own journey of discovering the key to authentically loving and accepting herself as she is. Bethany gives us a transparent and vulnerable look at the courage it takes to move from a life of despair to one of joy. Through Bethany's memoirs, we can learn that self-love is not selfish, but rather self-care. She reveals the keys to being an authentic leader in our own life through authentically living our truth. Join her on her journey of transformation and be prepared to have your heart transformed in the process."

~ Kimberly Schulte, Life and Business Transformational Coach, www.kimberly-schulte.com

"Bethany shares a powerful, empowering, and gutsy raw look at what her journey has been by peeling back the onion and stepping into vulnerability, imperfection and authenticity. As scary and uncomfortable as the process was for her and others facing similar journeys, the freedom that is waiting for her and others makes it all worth it! Faith in action — this book is the life transformation guide for woman looking to find their true wonderfully imperfect selves."

~ Jen McDonough "The Iron Jen", Amazon Top 100 Author to *Living Beyond Rich, Living Beyond Awesome, & 5 Minutes a Day to Living Beyond Rich*, Motivational Storyteller, & Coach, www.TheIronJen.com

"What does it mean to truly KNOW the unfathomable love of God and learn to fall in love with who you are as you begin to see yourself in the mirror of His eyes? Bethany poignantly and openly shares her journey to self-love. This book will allow you to look deeply into the eyes of the One who adores you."
~ Centa Terry, Facilitator, Dynamic Discipleship, Inc.
www.centaterry.com

"As women, how often do we dare to LOVE? How often do we dare to be hurt by love? How often are we willing to share the journey of wounds publicly, so others can be encouraged to love again? Bethany's *Cherished: One Woman's Journey to Love and Be Loved* does just that for us! Just like many of us, her "tough" outwardly appearance has been her "protection" cover up for long years, till she came to encounter with herself through her CREATOR's lens (HE is LOVE himself.), finally she has courage to LOVE again! I highly recommend you to allow yourself to visit her journey, and maybe, have a good ride together!"
~ Kelly Baader, Author of Amazon Bestseller *A Little Girl Called Grace*, Certified Business Coach | Speaker | Trainer with John C Maxwell Team, www.KellyBaader.com

"Bethany has written an incredibly practical book straight from her heart. Readers will know Bethany and will hear of her temptation to live "in control." The heart of letting go is the message of her book. You will learn freedom. At its best. His ways are always best. Thanks Bethany for your heart poured out on paper."
~ Jenny Price, Author of *7 Shifts Moving You Forward Faster*, Life Coach at Every Day Life Line Coaching Services,
www.iwokeupyesterday.com

"I really enjoyed Bethany Connor's book *Cherished: One Woman's Journey to Love and Be Loved*. Each chapter focuses on a topic related to love — what ends up happening is that you learn several aspects as well as engaging stories — thoughts, hope, & encouragement. It is like the book ignites you to find what is inside of you that you treasure most about your life related to love, and to take action on it. The book is full of heart warming and touching stories. You will feel better after reading this book. I can see this book easily rise to best seller status!"

~ John Ramsey, Speaker/ Spiritual Teacher/Life Coach, Targeting Excellence, Spirit Driven Coaching, www.johnexcellence.com

"Bethany masterfully weaves her own authentic story alongside an epic need that confronts every woman's heart. *Cherished* guides readers through their hurts and into the healing arms of the God who made them."

~ Kary Oberbrunner, author of *The Deeper Path* and *Your Secret Name*, www.karyoberbrunner.com

"In *Cherished*, you'll learn how Bethany Connor turned failure into freedom. This book will challenge you to re-evaluate everything that you have held to be true and realign it with the Truth that is within you. Reading this book is like taking a warm bath; it nurtures you from the inside-out"

~ Joel Boggess, host of Finding your Voice and author to three books

DEDICATION

"A leader interferes in other people's lives and causes them to do what they otherwise would not do towards what matters to them."
~ Brian Klemmer

This book is dedicated in loving memory to Brian Klemmer. Thank you Brian for interfering in my life and allowing me to wake up to the greatness within me.

CONTENTS

FOREWORD

The first time I met Bethany Connor was at a retreat center in the Texas Hill country where she was serving as a camp counselor for our church youth group. I was only there for a day, but had the privilege of sitting next to Bethany at lunch. After enjoying some good Texas barbeque, Bethany and I had a chance to talk. I learned she was a career-minded officer in the US Army responsible for training all the new nurses. It was clear she was good at what she did and passionate about making a difference.

I also discovered Bethany was a student of leadership, well read and articulate. She was a leader of leaders. I was impressed. Back at the office I mentioned to some of my colleagues that one day the world would hear from Bethany. I was right. Bethany has a story that needs to be told. But her message in her new book, *Cherished: One Woman's Journey to Love and Be Loved* is not what you may think.

Bethany was a strong, successful career woman. But she was also broken. Her desire to love and be loved eluded her. Life experiences crippled her spirit. To cope, Bethany masked her pain with hard work. But underneath the mask were unhealed wounds, unmet needs and depression. Eventually the pain of emotional brokenness led Bethany to "unmask" and engage in honest introspection. She embraced the hard work of RECOVERY — not from alcohol or drugs, but from hurt, disappointment and brokenness.

It was a painful journey for Bethany, but eventually she found her path to loving herself, and being loved by God. Personally, I'm glad she has chronicled her life events into this powerful story of recovery. I believe her journey will inspire hope in all those who read it!

~ David Saathoff
Senior Pastor, San Antonio CityChurch
www.sacitychurch.com

PREFACE

I've always been a very private person. I am an introvert who likes to keep to myself and keep a low profile. At least that's what I've always told myself. What I've learned is that what I was telling myself wasn't actually the truth. The things I had been telling myself my whole life were the very things that were holding me back and keeping me from living out my greatness.

For years I lived on autopilot. I kept busy doing. Busyness served me well in life. Even when I was in high school, my schedule was packed. During the school week, I would go from one event to another. After school, I would attend student council, then basketball practice, and swim team practice. When I finally got home late in the evening, I would have just enough time to eat dinner, do my homework, then go to sleep so I could do it all again the next day. On the weekends, I worked two jobs. I would wake up at 5:00 in the morning, work an eight-hour shift at my first job, then drive across town to work another eight-hour shift at my next job. I thrived on being busy. It served me well then, just as it served me well into my adulthood.

I took those character traits that had worked well for me growing up and brought them with me into my career as an Army Nurse. My work ethic and busyness was rewarded and it was rewarding. It was rewarded through accolades from patients, co-workers, and supervisors. It was reflected in my high evaluations and in the awards that I received. It gave me a sense of self-worth. It made me feel appreciated, admired, and needed. It was a win-win. The Army got a hard worker who threw herself into her job and did everything with excellence and I got to feel important, loved, and needed.

Those weren't the only reasons that I threw myself into my work. There was actually a much bigger reason — to protect myself and keep myself from getting hurt again. When I was a young lieutenant, I met a fellow officer, fell in love, and got married. I was young, naïve, and (although I didn't know it at the time) insecure. The relationship ended in betrayal and hurt. After that relationship, I decided that I was never going to let myself be hurt again. I numbed the pain by keeping busy and throwing myself even deeper and even more passionately into my work. I could control my work environment and create walls of safety for myself.

In order to protect myself from getting hurt and in order to live out the perception of what an Army officer should be, I put on masks. Masks made me look good. They allowed me to exemplify military bearing. They also kept me safe; they kept me from being known, which kept me from being rejected or getting hurt and this was a risk I wanted to avoid at all costs.

There was the mask of perfection — of having it all together. I had high (impossible) expectations for myself and for other people.

There was the mask of being unbreakable — I was tough, I could handle whatever came my way. I did not feel; feelings were weak. They were okay for other people, but not for me. I focused on the work that needed to be done — the tasks at hand and how to improve what was being done and make it more efficient.

There was the mask of independence. I didn't need anyone else. I could handle life on my own.

And there was one of my most favorite masks — the mask of control. I was in control and held the keys to what was next in my life. The illusion of having everything in control helped me to feel like I had power; power to protect myself and power to ensure that things were executed the way that I thought that they should go.

Over the past three years, everything that had previously worked for me started to unravel from the inside out. As the layers of masks were peeling off, the pain surfaced, and the truth came through. Everything that I thought was the truth, I realized was no longer the truth. I lost control of everything that I thought I had control over and I spiraled down into a severe depression. The busyness worked as a coping tool, but left me feeling hollow and empty. I felt hopeless, helpless, and powerless.

This book is my journey through those three years of deep pain and deliberate self-discovery. I share this journey with you, so that you will know that you are not alone and so that you will know that there is hope. The following pages will take you through my thought processes, my internal struggles, my revelations, and my breakthroughs.

Follow me on the journey as I live in the question by asking myself questions and pushing through until the answers reveal themselves. Join me as I learn to love myself and to let myself be loved by God. My hope is that through walking beside me on my journey, perhaps you may begin your own journey of self-discovery.

PART I

Love Hurts

CHAPTER 1:

Sunglasses

"Man's mind, once stretched by a new idea,
never regains its original dimensions."
~ Oliver Wendell Holmes

In the spring of 2009, I started a journey that forever changed the trajectory of my life as I knew it. It was a journey deep within my soul-a journey of self-discovery. At the time I was just finishing up my third year of being stationed in Hawaii. Just like every other Sunday morning I went to my church, The Ark Christian Center, in Kaneohe, HI. I loved my church because it was like family. Everyone would greet me by name and with hugs and I truly felt like I was part of their Hawaiian "Ohana" (family).

That Sunday in particular, we had a guest speaker visit named Brian Klemmer. He was a funny and engaging speaker. I remember him getting up on stage wearing a big pair of sunglasses and sharing this story:

He asked the question, "What if you were born with a pair of green sunglasses on? You didn't know that you were wearing them. But because you were wearing them, everything that you saw in your life was seen in shades of green. And you have a really good friend who was wearing a white shirt. As you and your friend were discussing the color of his shirt, you got into an argument. You knew beyond a shadow of a doubt that your friend's shirt was green and nothing that he said or did was going to change your mind.

What if your friend, loving you and wanting you to know the truth called you up every day for a year telling you that his shirt was white? Would that convince you that his shirt was not green? As long as you kept those sunglasses on, that was your reality.

What if in a split second, one day, you became aware of those sunglasses? Once you became aware of them, then you could choose your experience. You could experience life through the green sunglasses that you have always known and are comfortable with, or you could create a new experience."

With awareness comes choice.

This concept intrigued me…was I wearing sunglasses that I wasn't aware of? What if I didn't know what I didn't know? As he continued speaking he started talking about events that occur in our lives and meaning that we create around those events. He explained that people could have the same event and each make it mean something different.

Then he said something that blew my mind! He said, "Facts don't mean anything!" What? Facts don't mean anything? Of course they do. Facts are facts. They are indisputable, aren't they?

What if facts were just facts, they were just events that happened? What if the meaning I made up about the event was just that, something I made up? That would mean that I could change the meaning and change my experience.

What? This is craziness! This is against everything that I've ever experienced! All the hurts and disappointments that I've had in my life, are you telling me that I just made that stuff up, that I *wanted* to suffer!?! I could tell you hands down how I was the victim in my marriage with a husband who was unfaithful to me and here I was seven years later alone and unwilling to be hurt again. That is a fact!

Or was it? Maybe the fact was that my ex-husband had cheated on me. That's it. That is the fact. Me being alone and not wanting to get hurt, that was the experience that I chose to create.

What? I didn't choose to have my husband cheat on me. No, I didn't choose that, but what did I choose? I chose to marry a man I knew wasn't a "Christian" and with whom I would not be able to share that very important part of my life. I chose to have sex with him before I was married which was against everything that I was taught and believed. I chose to trust and believe in him even when circumstances should have put up red flags. I chose to believe that he would be different from how he was brought up and what was role modeled for him. I believed I could help change him into the better person that he said that he wanted to be.

Wow, huge revelations! Who is Brian Klemmer and what is this line of thinking?

After church, I got to meet Brian Klemmer in person. He signed his book for me and invited me to attend a problem-solving seminar that he was having the next night for free since I had purchased his book. Well, I love learning new things and my curiosity was peaked, so a friend and I went to listen to him speak the next evening.

That night he spoke of a secret success formula and actually had audience members demonstrate the veracity of the formula. He spoke of achieving goals, of his 500-year plan, and generously gave away books, products, and a $100 dollar bill. Again, I was left thinking, who is this guy and what is this all about? Continuing to be intrigued and wanting to learn more, I signed up for the weekend seminar that was scheduled in downtown Waikiki the next month.

I arrived at the weekend seminar with no idea what to expect. It was an experiential workshop different than anything I had ever attended before, and it was very much outside of my comfort zone. There were incredible interactive exercises that had much more meaning than the exercises themselves. That weekend I learned to be uncomfortable with myself, so that I could eventually feel comfortable with myself again.

During the weekend workshop I learned about the art of listening and that there were three ways to listen: to agree, to disagree, or to be with. Prior to that weekend, I thought that I was a good listener. Officers would often come to me with their problems and challenges and I would listen and mentor them.

Was I really listening though? No, if I was to be honest with myself I wasn't actually listening. What was I doing then while I feigned listening? Well, it depended. If I agreed with the person, I would be shaking my head up and down and at the first available opportunity, I would jump in to share an experience in my life that confirmed what they were saying and why I agreed with them. If I didn't agree with that person, while they were talking I would be formulating in my head all the reasons I did not agree with them, and at the first available opportunity I would jump in to share the experiences in my life that confirmed why I did not agree with them.

That weekend I became acutely aware of how poorly I really did listen. I thought back to interactions that I had with some of my officers and I noticed how I cut them off by saying, "I know." Had I really listened I would have chosen to "be with" those officers, to listen to what they had to say and seek to fully understand their perspective. Instead, what I chose to do was to interrupt and act like I already knew what they were going to say. After all, I outranked them and had much more life experience than they did and I wanted to be seen as being knowledgeable so that they would respect and revere me.

There was a session that weekend on personality types and how to interact with other personalities. I have had experience with many personality assessment programs before and they have always fascinated me. This was a new one that I hadn't previously experienced. Participants were separated into one of four categories: controller, promoter, analyzer, and supporter.

I really enjoyed this exercise. As a group we came up with all the characteristics that exemplified our group: likes, dislikes, focuses, strengths, weaknesses, and motivations. I, of course, was a controller. I knew exactly which category I fit into and was very much a leader on this team. I was passionate about doing this exercise and tracking all the answers neatly on the butcher block so that we, as a group, could share all about our awesome personality type!

As each group shared, I noticed within myself different responses regarding my personal thoughts, feelings, and experiences about each group. Promoters were fun! I loved promoters and loved to be around them. They were the life of the party, had fun ideas, and always had lots of energy. My ex-husband was a promoter. I think that was a big part of what attracted me to him. I loved that he was fun and I felt like I was not fun. Fascinatingly, I felt attracted to promoters because I felt they were what I was not, so I have looked to them to fill what I felt I was missing in myself.

I really appreciated analyzers. I liked to execute and make things happen, but all the behind the scenes research felt kind of boring and monotonous to me. Analyzers did all the hard, behind the scenes research work, and then I could use all their hard work to help execute, make things happen, and bring ideas into reality. I also loved that analyzers were good at money. Money stuff bored me. Don't get me wrong, I liked money. It was a nice tool to get things done, but it was really not all that important to me. I had always told myself that I was not good at money. I got bored at balancing checkbooks down to the penny. I was good at saving money, but found it a waste of time to spend all my time calculating my finances. I chose to leave all the hard thinking for the analyzers.

Supporters, now this was a category of people that just annoyed me. I did not understand supporters at all. They were into rainbows, butterflies, and kumbaya. I found them to be lazy, wishy-washy, and unproductive. I was all about productivity and making things happen. That is how I, as a "controller," derived my self-worth: from productivity, for being praised for my accomplishments, and for excelling as a leader. Why would anyone want to be anything but a controller? After all, we were the best at everything we did!

This weekend sunglasses were again brought up. I learned that 50% of all belief systems (sunglasses) are set between 0-4 years of age and that 30% of belief systems are set between the ages of four to eight. So, by the time children are eight years old, 80% of their belief systems are already set.

Holy cow! What did this mean for me? You mean to tell me that by the time I was eight years old, I had thought processes that were engrained so deeply within that they affected decisions that I was making today as a grown adult?

What were my sunglasses? This weekend I discovered a few more sets of my sunglasses:

~ I like to keep a low profile. I don't like attention and don't like to brag.

~ I don't like wasting time!

~ I am not fun.

~ I am not good at storytelling.

~ I like to know all the answers.

So, were these sunglasses bad? No, not necessarily. These were developed early on in my life and had served me well to get where I am today. However, previous to this weekend I did not know that these sunglasses existed. Because I didn't know that they existed, I thought that they were the truth and that was just the way life was. Now that I realize that I am wearing these sunglasses, I now have the choice of whether I want to continue to wear them or choose something different. How empowering!

At one point in the weekend, we played a game. As the facilitator was giving the instructions for the game, I remember thinking in the back of my head, "Really, a game? I am not playing a game. This game is pointless and a waste of my time." Of course, I went through the motions of the game, but I didn't engage and I certainly didn't lead. I did not like to waste my time and a silly game was not a good use of my time.

That evening the facilitator gave us "homework" related to our experience of the game. I remember writing down my answers for the homework and thinking that I pretty much got nothing out of it. The next morning people were given time to share their experiences of the game. As people started sharing, I started to realize that there was a lot more to the game than the game itself.

As the weekend closed, the facilitator gave us each a gift to remember the weekend by. The gift was related to the game. It turns out that the teachings of the whole weekend and behind the company itself had been based around the game that I had dismissed as silly and worthless. What a punch in the gut for me! Where else in my life was I choosing to shut down and not participate because I thought it was a waste of my precious time? Wow!

For me, the most empowering point of the weekend came around an exercise that we did that opened my eyes to victim mentality. Previously, I had never thought of myself as a victim. In fact, I had always been very conscious of how I wanted people to see me, and being a victim was not how I wanted to be seen. I wanted to be seen as tough, strong, stoic, as someone who could handle anything that came her way.

And yet, when I thought back to my marriage and how my husband had cheated on me, that was not my fault. I became a victim though, when I took the stance of it not being my fault. How confusing, but it wasn't my fault, was it? No, it wasn't my fault and what was my role? What choices did I make before, during, and after my relationship? How did I choose to respond (or not respond)?

Another profound concept I became aware of that weekend is the concept of the 3R's: resentment, resistance, and revenge. I knew these concepts quite well, especially the first two.

I had a lot or resentment towards my ex-husband. I felt as though he had wasted years of my life and I was very angry at him for that. I was angry at him for not being honest with me from the beginning of our relationship. I was angry at him for cheating on me. He had no reason to cheat on me, I was awesome, loyal, and completely faithful to him.

Not only was I angry at him, I was angry at the whole male species! As far as I was concerned all guys sucked and I was not going to be hurt again, no way! I knew exactly how to not get hurt again: by putting up a wall (resistance) and not letting any guy into my heart ever again! Vulnerability was weak and caused way too much pain. I would never let myself be vulnerable again, ever!

Chapter 2:

Tearing Down Walls

God has an amazing way of aligning things so that they work out serendipitously according to His plan. I decided to move forward to the next level of training offered. It just so happened that the next available class, held in San Francisco, corresponded with the dates that I was due to change my duty assignment. I took some leave on my way from Hawaii to San Antonio and had a stopover in San Francisco to attend the workshop.

I love leadership trainings and was looking forward to the adventure. I was moving into a nurse instructor position, so I figured I might even learn something that I could use in my classes with my students. And, I had to admit, I had actually gotten quite a bit out of the previous classes and I was curious what the next level entailed.

I arrived to the training, homeless with two suitcases and my computer bag in tow. I didn't know anyone else at the training. All I knew was that that was exactly where I needed to be. The first day of class, the three facilitators introduced themselves, as did their support staff. When the support staff stood up, they described themselves using contract statements, such as, "I am a passionate, strong, and joyful woman." They were very catchy.

I thought about what my contract statement would be if I were to have one. It would be something strong, like, "I am a confident, courageous, and independent woman." Those were characteristics that described me exactly. I would feel proud to stand up and share that as my contract statement.

As it would happen, I did get the opportunity to develop my individual contract statement while at that training. I wrestled with that process throughout the whole session.

You see, the contract statement described the qualities that I was choosing to step into throughout the week, qualities that were a stretch for me, outside of my comfort zone. The qualities that were outside of my comfort zone were qualities such as caring, vulnerable, trusting, and peaceful. These were not qualities that I wanted associated with me. As far as I was concerned, these qualities were weak and I wanted no part of them.

In one of the first exercises we did, the facilitator asked me, "What would happen if you stepped into vulnerability?" What a dumb question I thought; why in the world would I want to step into vulnerability? That is so weak.

As I continued the struggle of choosing my qualities, I sought out one of the facilitators during a break and I asked,

"What if you don't want certain qualities?" The facilitator responded, "It doesn't have to be either/or, you can have it all."

Well, I didn't want to have it all. There is no way that I wanted to be known for having weak qualities, especially trust and vulnerability. I had been vulnerable before and I had trusted before and it caused nothing but heartache and pain.

So instead, I worked on coming up with a strong contract statement, which would represent who I really was and what I wanted to portray. Something like, "I am a courageous and honest woman of integrity." Yes, that would be a good one. After all it takes courage to be vulnerable (not that being vulnerable is a quality that I would want) and to be honest with myself.

On the second day of class we had an exercise that didn't even seem like an exercise. I decided early on in the "exercise" that this wasn't really important and was a total waste of my time. (Sound familiar?)

While other people talked among themselves, argued with each other, and tried to create consensus, I checked out. For a while, I amused myself by watching all the people interacting with one another. I was judging them for what they were saying and the decisions that they were making, but not offering the clearly right answer that I knew I had.

That got boring after a while, so I went to the side of the room and started doing push-ups. I am in the Army after all, that would be a way to help me stay in shape and blow off some steam and boredom from these clearly inadequate leaders. I mean shoot; we do this leadership stuff all the time in the Army. I could so easily bring this room together, direct them, and show them the right way to get things done, but since I decided this exercise was meaningless that would be a waste of my time and energy.

Yes, that was my thought process. What other times in my life have I "checked out" when things weren't "important" to me? When in life have I chosen not to step forward into a leadership position, even though God has clearly given me the skills, talents, and abilities to excel in that area? Where else in life do I pass judgment on other people, waiting for them to fail instead of helping them?

During one of the days we played a game. I decided this time I would actually participate in the game. The concept seemed fun and I could excel as a leader. There were a lot of rules in the game. I listened to the instructions and they seemed easy enough. This was going to be fun!

When it was my turn, I moved forward confidently knowing that I was going to represent my team well. Unfortunately, it didn't go as I had planned. I lost in the first round and was out for the rest of the game. Once I became disqualified, I was no longer a participant, nor was I allowed to see the game continue and had to follow the rules for disqualified team members. Well, that stunk — that was not the way I had planned it to go.

I decided that it didn't really matter anyway. It was just a silly game after all. It wasn't important. I thought about how I had lost, I did it wrong because I hadn't been paying close enough attention during the directions. I had thought to myself, "Oh, I know how to do that," so I didn't actually pay attention to exactly how it was supposed to be done. Where else in life did I not pay attention to detail? What other times in my life had I failed at something and after the fact had decided it was not actually that important?

It was also during this training that I first heard of the concept "competing commitments." A competing commitment is when I say that I want one thing, but I also want something else that keeps me from the thing that I say I want because I want to be seen a certain way. I identified quite a few competing commitments in my life. I was committed to the goals that I said that I wanted, but I was also committed to appearing:

~ KNOWLEDGEABLE so that I would be ADMIRED
~ CONFIDENT so that I would be RESPECTED
~ CARING so that I would be APPRECIATED
~ POSITIVE so that I would be ADMIRED
~ FRIENDLY so that I would be LIKED
~ ORGANIZED so that I would be NEEDED
~ TOUGH so that I would be SAFE
~ INDEPENDENT so that I would be SAFE
~ STRONG so that I would be RESPECTED
~ GENEROUS so that I would be APPRECIATED

Wow, so I say I want one thing, but then I sabotage what I say I want, so that I can be seen a certain way? Fascinating, I never knew that about myself. Some of these were tough pills to swallow. I always thought that I was a positive, caring, friendly, generous, and organized person. But really deep down inside, I had ulterior motives for acting that way.

So did that mean that I was a fake? Did I act this way just so that I could be admired, appreciated, liked, and needed? In my job as an Army officer, I always portrayed myself as being confident, knowledgeable, tough, independent, and strong. But did I act that way so I could be admired, respected, and safe? Whoa! My mind was blown! What was I supposed to do with this new found knowledge? Was I going to stop being nice to people now that I knew my motives behind why I did what I did?

At one point in the five day training, I had a significant "aha" moment. During one exercise, I was asked to share something that I didn't want anyone else to know about me. My big "secret" was that I had been divorced.

After my divorce, I did not talk about having been married. I didn't want people to know and, honestly, I didn't want to think about that period in my life. It had hurt too much and I had never dealt with the hurt. So I kept staying really busy, being distracted by work, and moving forward with my life.

I had been brought up in a "Christian" household. I knew from a young age that divorce was not authorized in a marriage. I had told my ex-husband very clearly before we got married that "I did not believe in divorce" and "divorce was not an option." He knew this going in, yet still chose to act against my clear proclamations of my expectations for our marriage.

My big "aha" moment was that the reason I felt so shameful about having been divorced was because of my pride. When I filled out any paperwork that asked my marital status, instead of checking "divorced," I would check "single." I was so angry at my ex-husband for having given me the stigma of being "divorced". I was mad at him for cheating on me. I was mad at him for not manning up and staying in the marriage that he had committed to even after I had "forgiven" him. I was mad at him for ruining all the hopes and dreams that we had planned for our future together.

Yes, I was heart-wrenched that he did not love me enough to stay faithful to me; that had hurt, but the hurt had faded. This was seven years later and I still kept the "secret" of being divorced close to my chest. Why did I feel so much shame regarding this stigma? It was commonplace nowadays, even for "Christian" marriages to end in divorce.

But I didn't want that label. I never wanted that label; and now I had that label and it hurt my pride. I had wanted to have the perfect marriage, the perfect life, and the happily ever after ending; and once that dream had been shattered, so was my future.

By the end of the five-day training, I had decided that I was tired of keeping up the walls I had built. It had been over seven years and I was tired of being angry and lonely. I started to realize that the same walls of protection that I had put up to keep myself from getting hurt, also kept the good out, too — love, joy, intimacy, and connection.

I chose to step into being a courageous, trusting, vulnerable, and caring woman. Was I scared? Absolutely. I did not want to get hurt again; but I also didn't want to keep my life on hold anymore. It was time for me to tear down the walls.

CHAPTER 3:

Taking a Chance with Love

*"But what if it doesn't work out? Ah, but
what if it does."*
~ Peter McWilliams

The last night of the workshop in San Francisco a group of us went into the city to hang out. At the end of the night one of the guys from the group walked me back to my room. He texted me later that night, typing, "You are an amazing woman." I remember thinking, how does he know that? We had just hung out down at the pier and went out to dinner.

As we traveled back to our respective cities, we started texting back and forth. I received another text from him as I was boarding for the second leg of my layover. I read the text as I boarded the plane and my eyes started to water. I remember telling God, "God, I don't know if I'm ready for this." We continued to connect by sending upwards of thirty texts a day to one another and talking on the phone in-between. I was enjoying the connection, but still remained stand-offish.

After three weeks, I let my family know very nonchalantly that I had been talking to a guy. It was no big deal (after all I like to keep a low profile) and it would keep me from getting disappointed if nothing came of it. During one of our phone conversations I told him I was afraid (of taking a chance with us).

He said to me, "What if?"

What if, huh?

What if I took a chance with him?

One of the things I had learned at the training in San Francisco was to live out of my heart instead of from my head. Ever since my divorce, I had hardened my heart and I lived out of my head. My head was rational; it was realistic. It would not let me get hurt and I did not want to get hurt, so it was safe living out of my head. I decided that I would take a chance. What if it did work out? What if he was the one that I had waited for all this time? What if I finally might get my happily ever after?

When my car arrived to Dallas from Hawaii, I asked him if he would fly down and take a road trip with me. He said yes. I felt nervous when I was looking for him at the airport. I didn't know if I would be able to recognize him and I was second-guessing why I had even asked him in the first place. When I saw him I remembered how fun and handsome he was and felt glad that I had asked him after all.

The six-hour drive from Dallas to San Antonio just flew by! That first weekend together felt amazing! We just totally connected and had so much fun. I felt so happy and content.

He flew down again when I was moving into my house. Every time we were together it just seemed like things got better and better. I remember one night we started laughing- my spirit had never felt so happy and so free! There was a sparkle in my eye and a spring in my step! I was starting to fall in love!

As he was helping me unpack some of my boxes, I remember him asking me if I would change my last name to his. Well, gosh, I had not even thought of that. Everyone in the Army knew me by my last name. I was well known and well respected; I wasn't sure. What I was sure of though was that he was "the one." I had finally met a Christian guy, who was handsome, funny, and adored me! I was ready to elope with this guy. He was the one I had been waiting for! I just wanted to be together and have our future together start as soon as possible!

CHAPTER 4:

Pain and Confusion

Living in different states, we took turns flying back and forth to visit one another. We had started training for a marathon together, so we trained separately and kept each other up to date. After one of my Saturday morning long runs, I gave him a call to chat on my drive back home. He played basketball on Saturday mornings and had injured his knee that morning. He ended up needing surgery. A few weeks later, he had his surgery. The weekend after his surgery, I flew up to see him. It felt so good to spend time with him in person again.

The first night we enjoyed each other's company.

The second day we went to a birthday party for his niece and I met his family. I spent most of the time with his mom and sisters-in-law, while he hung out with the guys. "So this was going to be my new family," I thought. I noticed as he was with his family, he was not as affectionate toward me. He must just be acting macho in front of his brothers.

The next day he was very distant and did not want to be alone together. I didn't understand. I could tell that he was pulling away. As he was driving me back to the airport I kind of thought that he didn't want to be with me any longer. I was actually surprised when he asked me if I would come back for Thanksgiving. Maybe I had just been imagining things? I just chalked his distant behavior up to him not feeling good after the surgery.

After I got home from the trip, he gradually started distancing himself more and more. Thirty texts a day dwindled down to one every three days. Then he stopped returning my phone calls. What had I done wrong to push him away like this? Why was he ignoring me?

I remember telling him during one of our phone calls, "I don't feel like I'm a priority to you."

I wanted to be a priority. Why didn't he listen? I was telling him what I needed. We had been reading *The Five Love Languages*[1] book together. When I finished the book, I was excited to tell him what I had realized about myself and I wanted to hear what he had discovered.

He didn't want to hear and he didn't really want to talk about it. He said that he would use what he learned with his clients in his work as a counselor.

I was trying to figure out what had gone wrong and why he was distancing himself from me. Maybe it was because I was still training for the marathon and he wasn't able to anymore. I knew that he had some financial stuff going on. Maybe it was because of the pressure of that. And I'm sure it didn't help him to feel any better since I had just bought a new house and was remodeling it. Maybe that was why. I wanted him to know that it didn't matter. When stuff like this came up, we could work through it together. The most important thing was that we were together and we had one another. I wanted to talk, to find out why he was pulling away, and why he was ignoring me. It felt very personal — that I wasn't desirable, that I wasn't worth loving, that I wasn't worth fighting for…

I flew up to see him over Thanksgiving. He had asked me, "Are you sure you want to still come?" Yes, I wanted to still come! I wanted to find out what in the world was going on and I needed to talk face to face. I just knew when he saw me, all his feelings would come back and he would remember the love that we had shared. He picked me up at the airport and gave me an awesome hug. We talked on the ride back to his house.

As we were driving, I reached over and rubbed the back of his head. He used to love that. He pulled away when I did that. "What was wrong?" I asked.

He said to me, "I don't know, I'm just numb."

Okay? So what did that mean?

We got to his house and he proceeded to ignore me. He was reading his mail, staying on the other side of the room, it was as though I wasn't even there. After an hour of being ignored, I decided that he was making it easy for me. I called my sister and had her reschedule my return flight to fly out the next morning on Thanksgiving Day.

All night I sat on his couch and just cried. What in the heck had happened? Why was he ignoring me? It hurt so much to be ignored. At least he could have let me know what happened. He could tell me that he didn't want to be together anymore or that he had found someone else. Instead, nothing, he just shut down and ignored my very existence.

The next morning as he drove me to the airport I remember saying, "What in the world is God doing?"

He replied, "He is the only one who knows what He is doing."

CHAPTER 5:

Hold On

My parents had been visiting my house while it was being remodeled. They picked me up from the airport. I remember riding in the car and I heard God's voice say to me, "Nothing that you do or say is going to affect the outcome."

Talk about feeling helpless. I am a controller and I like to make things happen; I like to address things head on and here He was telling me there was nothing I could do.

So, what, I just trust God? Right after saying that, I heard His voice say to me, "You flying to see him and coming back had to happen. I am so excited! It is going to be so amazing!!"

Okay, seriously God? It's going to be amazing? It doesn't feel very amazing. In fact, it pretty much sucks. You're telling me that there is nothing I can do to affect the outcome and that my life is going to be awesome? Well, it sure doesn't feel awesome! It feels like I've been rejected! I feel unappreciated, unloved, and unwanted! Why is it that guys don't want to stay with me? What do I do wrong? What's wrong with me? Why aren't I worth staying with?

From that day forward and for the next year and a half, I cried. I cried in the shower, I cried on my drive into work, I cried on my drive home from work, and I cried myself to sleep at night.

During the day I kept my game face on at work. I threw myself into my work because that was what I was comfortable with and what I knew best. That is what I had done after my divorce and it worked well for me then. Throwing myself into my work kept me busy, kept me distracted, and it allowed me to focus on other people and other things. It allowed me to be productive, to have a functional purpose, and above all, to feel appreciated.

I had decided that I didn't want to give up on "us" and "our relationship." I thought back to all the amazing memories that we had had together, to the good times that we had shared, and how it felt when we had been together. He had given me a taste of something amazing! Over and over I played back in my mind the times we had shared together. My heart swelled with joy at the memories and then crashed into despair once again when I realized that he had taken his love away.

I thought back to all of our times together, trying to figure out what went wrong. I wanted to figure out what his thinking was. I wanted him to know that I was not giving up on us and that we were worth fighting for. I would want someone to fight for me, because I'm worth fighting for. I wanted to give him the same kind of love that I wanted to receive; loyal, unconditional, and never ending. I had convinced myself that he was just going through personal stuff that he needed to work through.

As much as it hurt, I would give him the time and space he needed, so that he would eventually come back to his senses and realize what an amazing future we could have together!

CHAPTER 6:

Never Say Never

After about 10 months of crying, I started to lose my "game face" at work. As an Army Officer, I always took pride in maintaining my Army bearing. I had always kept my personal life separate from my work. No one needed to know if I had something going on at home. It was my responsibility to set the example for young officers on how to maintain military bearing at all times.

It was especially critical in the job I was currently serving in, as I had interaction with all the brand new nurses entering the Army. They needed to see someone who was strong, confident, who had it all together, and who could teach them how to do the same.

When I found myself tearing up at work, I desperately, yet reluctantly sought out help. As a nurse I knew the importance of therapy and medication to help people through times in their lives. I absolutely supported people in going those routes, but *I* didn't need medication and *I* didn't need therapy. Yet, at that point, I knew I was desperate and couldn't do it on my own. Stepping beyond my pride, I went to see my provider, got on some anti-depressant medications, and started looking for a counselor.

It felt kind of ironic when I started looking for a counselor. My ex-boyfriend had been a counselor. I remember one of our conversations, when he told me, "I would never be your counselor."

I had responded very cocky and full of confidence, "I would never need a counselor." Famous last words!

Until I started looking for a counselor, I never realized how hard it was to find one. Initially, I started looking outside of the military for a counselor. I work in the medical field and I didn't need the military to know about my personal issues. It was bad enough that I was already being seen and medicated for depression. That is something that I had not wanted on my record. Even though we're encouraged to be seen and treated for psychiatric issues, the unwritten rule that I told myself was: it's not okay.

I found a "Christian" counselor, not far from where I lived, so I made an appointment with her to be seen. I wanted to find someone who had a similar worldview as me. In our session, I talked with her about how I was walking in faith in regards to this relationship. She told me that I was not being rational. She said that I was welcome to come back, but that I was fine; I had just prolonged grief. I appreciated that she thought I was fine, yet I knew that I wasn't.

The next time I went in to see my provider for a follow up, he asked how the counseling was going. I shared my experience. He encouraged me to be seen by someone there in the clinic. I knew I needed something, so I agreed.

The next counselor that I saw was a civilian counselor who worked in the military clinic. I was in uniform when I went to see her. When I am in uniform, I always put on my "military Bethany" persona. The military Bethany is tough. She maintains her military bearing and does not cry in uniform. I talked with the counselor sharing with her a little bit about my situation. I was very careful about sharing too much, because I did not want things in my record and I didn't know how safe it would be share. To my relief she ended up talking most of the time. She let me go and said that I was fine. It was just work stress going on and I was welcome to come see her again. Phew, no thanks!

At the next follow up visit with my provider, he asked me again about seeing a counselor. I shared my experience. He told me he knew someone whom he thought would be a good fit with me and encouraged me to make an appointment. With a bit of hesitation, I made an appointment for an upcoming Monday.

The Friday evening before my appointment, I was finishing up in the office and looking at the schedule for the next week. I was going to be out in the field doing training with my officers on Monday. There was no way for me to make it all the way back to the base in time for the appointment. Since the clinic was closed, I called and left a message as well as e-mailed the provider just to let them know I wouldn't be able to make it to the Monday appointment.

At the end of the week I came back to the office and was called in to see my supervisor. She let me know that the Company Commander had contacted her to let her know that I had missed my psychiatric appointment. Seriously!?!

That was *exactly* why I *did not* want to get counseling through the military! It was bad enough that I had to go get help to begin with. The last thing I wanted was to have my supervisors know that I was getting seen. Forget counseling, I was fine.

CHAPTER 7:

You Do Not Fear Me

During this time period God started speaking to my heart about the Fear of the Lord. One day in particular he spoke quite clearly, "Think back to your whole career. You only respected certain leaders. If you did not like them or agree with their philosophy, then you chose not to respect them in your heart. This is not just with work, but with your Pastor as well. You also do it with me. You do not fear me. I put every leader in the position that they are in over you. It is your God given responsibility to honor and submit to those in authority over you, for I have put them there."

Ouch, this was true! I have had many leaders over the course of my career. There were certain leaders that I respected and admired. Usually those were leaders who were visionary, empowering, and fair in their execution. There were others who in my experience were toxic, incompetent, out only for themselves, or to look good. For the latter leaders I chose to hold resentment against them, did not respect them, and was haughty in my heart towards them. Now, of course, that was not something that I let them know. I would be disingenuously respectful toward them, but in my heart I was at war toward them. During this season, God prompted me to read John Bevere's book, *Under Cover.*[2] Through that book and through God speaking to me, He made it very clear that he had placed every leader in authority over me and it was my God given responsibility to submit to their authority. I really wrestled with this one! I had all my justifications and my reasons for my resentment. I could give clear examples that justified my position. And yet, I was arguing with the God of the universe. Who do you think ended up being right?

God was right; I did not fear Him. In fact, I remember a particular instance, after He had brought my ex-boyfriend into my life. Things were going so well with him and I was so thankful that God had brought him into my life. I was so thankful that I remember saying in my heart, "Thank you God for bringing him into my life. Thanks, I got it from here!"

Seriously? "I got it from here?" Did I just tell the God of the universe that I didn't need His help? That I would let Him know when I needed Him? Talk about a haughty heart, and I called myself a "Christian?" What kind of Christian tells God that they've got it under control and they'll let Him know when they need something? Yes, that was me!

I knew that I was pretty awesome. I was very confident in myself, my strength, and my capabilities. I did work with excellence and I was very productive in everything I did. I would just keep moving forward with ideas, working hard, and before I knew it I could look back and see amazing things that I accomplished with my own strength. I kept my life very compartmentalized and I gave God His own compartment. I lived life in my own strength and let Him know if and when I needed Him (which wasn't very often because I was tough and could handle things on my own).

I didn't understand the concept of people "giving God the glory" first. I mean, I knew that we were "supposed to" do that and of course it sounded good, but honestly that is not the first thing that came to my mind when I received accolades. Sure, I knew that God was around, but what I accomplished, *I* accomplished. As much as I didn't like the limelight (as a part of my low profile sunglasses), I did enjoy the recognition and the appreciation. It felt good to be recognized for my accomplishments. It made me feel important, valued, appreciated, and needed. It fed my ego.

I remember talking on the phone one day to someone who lovingly spoke the truth to me. I was in the midst of my depression and I was crying on the phone with her. She said to me, "Whatever is keeping you there (being sad) must be pretty big."

I was still in victim mode at that time and did not understand what she was saying. As if I wanted to be sad. I didn't want to give up the hope of my ex-boyfriend and I getting back together. I wasn't going to give up on "us." I guess that was what was big, my desire not to give up. It wasn't until a year and a half later, when I was able to start seeing things a bit more clearly, that I realized what was really holding me back. She was right. It was really big. It was my ego! My ego, the thing that kept me the most stuck was my pride; wanting to look good, wanting to be right.

That is what kept me stuck in my depression and in my life.

Chapter 8:

Breakdown to Breakthrough

I worked really hard to maintain my game face, keeping busy with work, and moving forward with my life. Well, actually, work was my life. The challenge was that not only was I emotionally distraught by my personal life, but I was feeling a lot of pressure and having a hard time at work, not with my students, they energized me and kept me going, but behind the scenes.

One day, after a hard day at work, I remember telling God, "I am overwhelmed. I cannot possibly do what is expected of me. It is too much!"

God responded, "Exactly. I don't want you to do it on your own strength. You are so good at doing it all on your own, that I had to keep giving you more and more until you could no longer do it in your own strength. Now, give it *all* to Me and let Me do it through you."

As God would have it, my church happened to be doing a series on brokenness during this time frame. I remember Pastor Dave saying, "Brokenness comes in the areas of our strengths, not our weakness. Bring your strength under God's control; whatever is your strength, God wants you to bring it under His control."[3]

God then spoke to me, "Leadership is one of your strengths, Beth. I need you to bring the strength of your leadership under *my* control. Just like Peter, you are confident in your own strength. Give me your strength and you will be even more effective through *my* supernatural strength."

Release control? I couldn't possibly do that. I am wired to be a controller, to make things happen. If I released control, then what would I do, trust in God?

I could hear Pastor Dave, "Brokenness occurs when our will and our strength are given to Him."[4]

But if I gave my will, my strength, and my control over to God, then what would I have left? Nothing. I resisted. Oh, how I resisted. I couldn't possibly release control to God. Me being in control gave me purpose, meaning, a feeling of accomplishment and satisfaction. Without my control and my accomplishments defining me who would I be? I could hear Pastor Dave again, "Lean into the pain and let God do His work in your soul."[5]

Lean into the pain? But it hurts! It's too much. Lean into the pain? I don't like pain. God, why? Why does it hurt so much? Why do I have to be here in this season? I don't want to be here anymore. It hurts. It's too much. I just want this to be over and done with.

Because He loves us, God gives us painful seasons to test us. *"My child, don't reject the Lord's discipline and don't be upset when he corrects you. For the Lord corrects those he loves, just as a father corrects a child in whom he delights."* ~ Proverbs 3:11-12 NLT

So, God loves me that's why I have all this pain? What kind of love is that? That's the kind of love a Heavenly Father provides to a child that He cares about. But it didn't *feel* good. It didn't *feel* comfortable. It didn't *feel* like He cared.

Another Sunday, Pastor Doug continued talking about brokenness, "When you are broken, you are finally able to release...release control. Let go, but hold on to God... Humility and brokenness lead to restoration... It is broken people that God uses His power through."[6]

Just release? As if that's an easy thing to do. Release everything to God and just trust in Him? I didn't want to release. I didn't want to let go. I didn't want to give up.

I wanted to control the little that I felt I had left in my life. I did not trust anyone, let alone God. But what I was doing wasn't working. With me in control, look where I had gotten myself. I was depressed. I was stuck. I was overwhelmed. What if I did just let go and give it to God? I certainly didn't have anything to lose. I don't think I could feel much worse than I already did. What if brokenness did lead to restoration? What if the way to the other side of this season was by going through, by leaning in to the pain? What if through my brokenness God could use me? What if He could actually use all things for good and somehow used this awful season in my life for something *amazing*?

I remember talking with my friend Kelley one evening on the phone. Actually, it was more like I was sobbing on the phone and she was listening to me, praying with me, and speaking over my life.

She told me, "He is breaking you down so He can build you back up... Release everything! He wants ALL of you!... Sometimes you have to break down in order to break through... He wants to give you all your hearts desires... Remain steadfast... He wants to be real to you... It's a heart thing. He's trying to get to your heart... Having a real relationship with God is a heart thing... Cry out to Him so He can show himself... He will pour his spirit, life, energy, love, and power into you, but you have to release *everything*!"

What powerful words and what a powerful friend, to just be present with me and to speak over me, while I just wrestled with my "stuff." To release everything? Sounds easy. Yeah right! To release everything, that is what He wanted for me. He didn't want me carrying burdens anymore.

Then Jesus said, "Come to me, all of you who are weary and carry heavy burdens, and I will give you rest. Take my yoke upon you. Let me teach you, because I am humble and gentle at heart, and you will find rest for your souls. For my yoke is easy to bear, and the burden I give you is light." ~ Matt 11:28-30 NLT

As I chose to remain in struggle, God continued to speak to me. One morning as I was sitting outside by my pool, He spoke to me, "Bethany, think of the butterfly in its cocoon. It must struggle to get out of the cocoon in order to gain strength it needs to become a beautiful butterfly. If someone tried to help it out of the cocoon and it did not go through the process, then it would die and would not become the beautiful creation that it was meant to be."

It is the process of the struggle where strength and growth is born.

Yet another Sunday, Pastor Shad spoke, "Lean into the pain of brokenness."[7]

I was starting to hear a theme. Lean into the pain. "Okay, God, I'm leaning. What I'm doing isn't working, so I'm going to try it your way. I have nothing to lose and everything to gain."

I remember Pastor Shad saying, "What would somebody in your current circumstances do if they knew for certain that God was with them?"[8]

Wow, if I knew for certain that God was with me, would I be sad? If I knew beyond a shadow of a doubt that God was in control and I trusted Him, would I be stuck in despair and hopelessness?

If God was really in control, then I had absolutely nothing to worry about. If God was really in control, then what He planned to happen is going to happen no matter what.

And if I truly believe that and trusted in Him, how would I feel? I would feel excited, expectant, peaceful, and hopeful.

Wow, that would *feel* good!

PART II

Love Heals

CHAPTER 9:

The Truth

One summer afternoon as I was floating in the pool, relaxing and enjoying the beauty all around me, I had a profound revelation: The Word of God is *the Truth*. I had remembered hearing that in Sunday school while growing up, but it really didn't mean much to me at the time. But what if that is true? What if the Word of God is the Truth? That would mean that every word that is written in the Bible is true. It would mean that it stays constant, it does not change, and it does not lie. It would mean that all the promises that God spoke way back when are still true today.

"For the Word of God is alive and powerful. It is sharper than the sharpest two-edged sword, cutting between soul and spirit, between joint and marrow. It exposes our innermost thoughts and desires." ~ Hebrews 4:12 NLT

What if the Bible is my guidebook to live by? What if it has all the answers to everything that happens in my life?

"All Scripture is given by inspiration of God, and is profitable for doctrine, for reproof, for correction, for instruction in righteousness, that the man of God may be complete, thoroughly equipped for every good work." ~ 2 Timothy 3:16-17 NKJV

I remember Pastor Shad saying something one Sunday that really spoke to my heart. He said, "Sometimes we define God by our circumstances rather than by His promises."[9]

That's exactly what I had been doing. I had been looking at my circumstances and they were bleak. They were discouraging. What if instead of looking at my circumstances, I instead focused on God's promises?

"For all of God's promises have been fulfilled in Christ with a resounding "Yes!" And through Christ, our "Amen" (which means "Yes") ascends to God for his glory." ~ 2 Cor 1:20 NLT

What if life's circumstances were just a distraction? What if the devil loved to keep me focused on my life circumstances and my feelings instead of keeping my eyes on God and trusting His promises over my feelings?

"Your enemy the devil prowls around like a roaring lion looking for someone to devour. Resist him, standing firm in the faith." ~ 1 Peter 5:8-9 NIV

What if the devil is a liar? What if he does his best to keep me distracted by my feelings and the things of this world? What if that is his way of keeping me from God's best, by allowing me to stay stuck in my stuff and living in despair?

"He was a murderer from the beginning. He has always hated the Truth, because there is no truth in him. When he lies, it is consistent with his character; for he is a liar and the father of lies." ~ John 8:44 NLT

What if the Word of God is actually my weapon to fight against the devil with?

"For our struggle is not against flesh and blood, but against the rulers, against the authorities, against the powers of this dark world and against the spiritual forces of evil in the heavenly realms. Therefore put on the full armor of God, so that when the day of evil comes, you may be able to stand your ground, and after you have done everything, to stand. Stand firm then, with the belt of truth buckled around your waist, with the breastplate of righteousness in place, and with your feet fitted with the readiness that comes from the gospel of peace. In addition to all this, take up the shield of faith, with which you can extinguish all the flaming arrows of the evil one. Take the helmet of salvation and the sword of the Spirit, which is the Word of God." ~ Ephesians 6:12-17 NIV

What if Jesus was my role model for how to live and how to fight the devil? When Jesus had been in the desert for 40 days and had not eaten, the devil tempted Jesus and Jesus used the Sword of the Spirit (the Word of God) to fight against the devil. If Jesus is my role model, then I too am empowered to use the Sword of the Spirit to fight the lies of the devil with the Truth, God's Word.

If the Word of God is the Truth and I chose to believe this then the whole paradigm of my life would change. That would mean that I would make decisions based on the Truth of God's Word instead of the ever changing "truth" of my feelings and perceptions. And I would speak the Truth over my life with unwavering faith.

If the Bible is true, then I already know the end of the story. I have all the answers to the test of life. All I need to do is read the Bible, use it as my guidebook through life, and pray for God's guidance with the direction that I should go.

"Your Word is a lamp to guide my feet and a light for my path."
~ Psalm 119:105 NLT

CHAPTER 10:

Walking in Faith

"Through the intimacy of our relationship, you are being transformed from the inside out. As you keep your focus on Me, I form you into the one I desire you to be. Your part is to yield to My creative work in you, neither resisting it nor trying to speed it up. Enjoy the tempo of a God-breathed life by letting Me set the pace. Hold my hand in childlike trust, and the way before you will open up step by step."
~ Sarah Young, *Jesus Calling*

One morning God spoke to me very clearly regarding my haughty heart. He said to me, "Remember Jonah and the whale. You are in the whale right now. Jonah was prideful and was haughty in his heart. That is why he chose to be disobedient to what I was asking him to do. Even after he got out of the whale, he did not change. He was compliant and obedient, but in his heart he was not committed.

After I had compassion on the city, he went to the outskirts of the city and pouted. He was mad at me for having compassion on *my* children. He was a vessel. It is not up to him what I choose to do, I AM God. He chose to be a haughty and prideful vessel. I was still able to use him but not to his full potential. I then had compassion on him, even though his heart was being judgmental against me and my actions, and I gave him a tree to shade him. The next day I chose to take the tree away and, he was upset. He did nothing to deserve the tree or to maintain the tree. The tree was my gift to him.

I AM God. I choose to give and take away. Many times this is to help teach my children and to help them to grow. It is up to them though if they choose to lean in and learn from these experiences or to harden their hearts and become angry and judgmental. I gave you your ex-boyfriend. He was my gift to you and I took him away. Do not be mad at him; do not be mad at me. I did this for a reason. Do not try to figure out why, what was done wrong, or how to fix it. I AM God. I give and take away.

Trust in my Word, "All things work together for good for those who believe." This will work together for good, according to my plan for your life. Stay on the path. Walk in faith step-by-step, day-by-day. I will give you just enough light for the step that you are on. Trust, trust in Me. I will never leave you or forsake you. I am with you every step of the way. I am guiding you on this journey. Stay in My light. Stay in My love."

"And we know that God causes everything to work together for the good of those who love God and are called according to his purpose for them." ~ Romans 8:28 NLT

Throughout my journey, God has placed songs in my path that have spoken to me directly. One of these songs is, "Praise You in the Storm" by Casting Crowns.

> I raise my hands and praise the God
> who gives and takes away
> I'll praise You in this storm
> And I will lift my hands
> for You are who You are
> no matter where I am
> Every tear I've cried
> you hold in Your hand
> You never left my side
> And though my heart is torn
> I will praise You in this storm

"He gives and takes away." Sometimes people or things are taken from us and we don't understand why. I know that I didn't understand why, after having been lonely for so long, that God would bring someone into my life and give me a taste of something amazing, just to take it away again. I can't tell you how many hours and how much energy I spent trying to figure it out. What if God didn't want me to figure it out? What if all He wanted was for me to trust Him even when I didn't understand why? What if trying to understand was my human nature trying to retain some semblance of control? What if there are some things I may never understand this side of heaven? And, what if that's okay?

Praising God even in the midst of heartbreak and despair is not a natural tendency. I know for me it wasn't. When I was feeling sad, desperate, hopeless and unloved, I did not feel like praising God. But what if it is through praising God that I can push beyond "feelings" to the Truth?

"Then you will know the Truth, and the truth will set you free."
~ John 8:32 NLT

What if feelings are not the truth? What if feelings are a distraction? I'm not saying to disregard feelings completely. What if feelings are a good indicator, but a bad dictator? What if it is healthy for me to identify and acknowledge my feelings, but *not* healthy for me to let my feelings dictate how I respond to a situation? What if feelings can change? What if I could have power over my feelings, instead of letting my feelings have power over me? How would that feel?

For a good year and a half, I let my feelings have power over me. I kept myself stuck, by holding on to those feelings and believing them to be true. As I wallowed in my feelings of sadness, despair, and hopelessness, I let those feelings have power over me. Doing that did not serve me. In fact, doing that is what kept me stuck! I did not know another way though. All I knew was what I felt and I thought that what I felt was the truth because it was true to me.

One morning, I received an email devotional from Rick Warren with the following excerpt, "In dog obedience training, they put a dog at one end of a room and its master at the other end of the room, with a plate of food in the middle. And then the master calls the dog. If the dog eyes the food, he's a goner; he'll go straight for it. So they teach the dog to focus his eyes on the master. If the dog keeps his eyes on the master, he won't be tempted. Instead of heading for the food, he'll head straight to the master."[10]

After reading this, God spoke to me, "Bethany, keep your eyes on the master. I AM the author and perfector of your faith. Look above your circumstances; circumstances are just a distracter. Keep your eyes on me."

What if that was the key? What if every time I felt sad and I started to go down the rabbit hole of feeling sorry for myself and trying to figure out why, instead I moved my eyes from my circumstances to God? What if that helped me from keeping myself stuck? What if looking at God instead of my circumstances filled me with strength instead of despair? Well, it certainly couldn't hurt to try.

"We do this by keeping our eyes on Jesus, the champion who initiates and perfects our faith. Because of the joy awaiting him, he endured the cross, disregarding its shame. Now he is seated in the place of honor beside God's throne." ~ Hebrews 12:2 NLT

What if when I had self-defeating thoughts, where I was focused on trying to figure things out, replaying scenarios in my head, or feeling unloved and unlovable, I intentionally replaced those thoughts with the Truth of God's Word? What if I spoke God's Word and His promises over my life rather than my feelings or my circumstances? Would that make a difference in how I felt? Would that support me in moving forward instead of staying stuck? Well, what I had been doing wasn't working and I certainly didn't have anything to lose.

"We destroy arguments and every lofty opinion raised against the knowledge of God, and take every thought captive to obey Christ." ~ 2 Cor 10:5 ESV

Throughout this journey, God has revealed to me what it *really* means to walk in faith, by trusting God's Word, speaking God's Word, believing God's Word, and living by God's Word daily. His Word does not lie. It is Truth. I have learned to speak God's Word over my situation and to believe in his Word in spite of what the circumstances might seem. I know that God is working behind the scenes in the realm of what cannot be seen.

When Jesus was in the desert, He spoke God's Word against Satan. I too must speak God's Word, His Truth against the lies that the devil tries to make me believe. I choose to trust the Word and the Truth that has been revealed to me and to my heart.

CHAPTER 11:

It Doesn't Have to Look a Certain Way

"Expectation is the root of all heartache."
~ William Shakespeare

I think a big part of what's held me back over the past few years was me being tied to things looking a certain way. I wanted my ex-boyfriend and me to be together. I really thought he was "the one" and so us not being together meant that I would be alone forever. There were things at work that didn't turn out the way that I had thought they should. What ended up happening was not what I pictured happening, yet the outcome was the same, it was just different.

What if true freedom comes from surrender? I did not want to surrender. I did not want to give up and I did not want to release my illusion of control. What if it's not a matter of giving up, but matter a of letting go? What if I let go of pre-conceived notions of how things "should" be and accepted "what is." I didn't like "what is." I didn't want "what is."

I wanted something more, I had big dreams and visions of what my life should look like, what our life together should look like and "what is" didn't look anything like what I wanted. What if, in order to get to where I want to be, I must first acknowledge, accept, and be grateful for what is?

Oh, how I struggled with this concept. I have high expectations for myself and for other people. I always strive to be the best that I can be and expect that level of performance of other people. I am never satisfied with the status quo. I am always improving myself and systems within my realm of influence (whether that be personal or professional). I expect perfection. I strive for perfection. And what I find is that I am always disappointed. No one ever lives up to my expectations, including myself.

So, what then, I just have low expectations for people? Or better yet *no* expectations? That does not make any sense whatsoever and is totally against anything that I have ever learned in leadership or in life.

Having no expectations, the thought of it... I mean if I had no expectations then nothing would get accomplished. If I had no expectations then how would the people that I work with know how or what to accomplish? If I had no expecta-tions for myself then I would get nothing done and just be lazy. Is that true? What if by having pre-conceived expecta-tions it puts limits on people, including myself? What if I could encourage the same level of excellence through lever-aging people's strengths and creativity and collaborating to create a synergistic effect that doesn't limit the outcome to what I think it should look like? What if having no expecta-tions means that I would never be disappointed? What if I maintained an attitude of expectancy without expectations?

"When you allow the good things in life to become mere expectations to be fulfilled, you lose the joy of *expectancy*. Return your heart to the expectancy that comes with hopeful longing. When you default to the point of expecta-tions, your motivation is clouded. Allow your light of expectancy to shine today and look forward to what is to come." ~ Lisa Schilling

Have you ever heard the saying, "what you resist persists?" What if that was true? What if me resisting "what is," was keeping me stuck where I said that I didn't want to be? Well, I was tired of being stuck, so what did I have to do to stop resisting? I had to accept "what is;" "this is it and I'm satis-fied."

Well, I certainly didn't feel satisfied, but I was choosing to accept my reality of what was. I had to choose to accept that my ex-boyfriend had chosen not to be with me and not to communicate with me and be satisfied with "what was." I wasn't ready to feel grateful about it, but I was choosing to accept it.

One Sunday, Pastor Dave spoke of the story of David and Saul. He described the "Way of David" as "letting go." God promised David that he would become King, however David had to live in caves first, being chased by King Saul. I imagine, that as David was living in caves, he was wondering what the heck was going on. David became King as God orchestrated it and it likely didn't look like what David had imagined.

During this teaching session, God spoke to me, "Let go and let Me reveal your future as I have orchestrated it, not as you think it should go."

Okay, God, I willingly release my destiny to you. It doesn't have to look a certain way.

CHAPTER 12:

Forgiveness Is Freedom

"Forgiveness is about RELEASE. It has very little to do with feelings or even trust. It's simply a decision to let go of our disappointment and expectations for our own sake. When our response is bitterness and anger it can affect our entire outlook on life and consume our emotional and physical energy. To forgive is to boldly declare that your life does not belong to the offending party or the incident in your past." ~ Dr. Bill Maier

At one time during this process, I had to attend a conference for work. It just so happened that my ex-husband was also scheduled to attend that conference. I had not spoken with him in over five years and our last conversation did not end well. I remember saying to God, "Seriously, God? Do you really think I can handle this too?" I had no desire to see him and felt like I was not at a place emotionally that I could handle seeing him. But I knew that I needed to go to this training as a part of my job and I imagined that God had some reason for orchestrating this as he did.

It had been nine years since we had divorced and I was pretty much numb to what had happened. I had moved on and didn't even think about it anymore. I had really just pretended that part of my life didn't even exist and that worked for me. I still had mistrust toward the male species, which had worked well to protect me and keep me from getting hurt. Had I forgiven my ex-husband? Sure, I guess. I didn't hate him as much as I had; I was just numb toward him.

I remember when he first told me that he had cheated on me. The pain of betrayal shot so deeply through my heart. I was so angry at him. I wanted to know every detail; who, when, and why. He told me what I wanted to hear. It sucked hearing it. Knowing those details filled my mind with mental images that did not serve me. I became jealous, mistrusting, and hateful. I turned into someone that I didn't recognize and that I didn't want to be. My heart filled with anger and bitterness towards him and towards every single woman that he had slept with.

The challenge with bitterness and unforgiveness is that it eats away on the inside of us. The bitterness and anger that I carried inside myself didn't affect him. He had moved on with his life. It had affected me. It kept me from living and truly experiencing life. I had put up a wall of protection to keep me from getting hurt by anyone ever again. The problem was that the wall that was keeping out the pain was also keeping out the joy. It was effective and it was keeping me from truly living.

I ended up talking with my ex-husband one day after the conference. Through that interaction with him, I was actually able to truly forgive him for the first time. I finally felt a peace within and a freedom to wish him well. Ironically the same day that I made peace with my ex-husband was the day that I started a Celebrate Recovery class at my church. I knew absolutely nothing about the class. This was the beginning of my journey of forgiveness.

CHAPTER 13:

Peeling Back the Onion

"The holiest men, the most free from impurity, have always felt it most. He whose garments are the whitest, will best perceive the spots upon them. He whose crown shineth the brightest, will know when he hath lost a jewel. He who giveth the most light to the world, will always be able to discover his own darkness. The angels of heaven veil their faces; and the angels of God on earth, his chosen people, must always veil their faces with humility, when they think of what they were. As you grow downward in humility seek also to grow upward, having nearer approaches to God in prayer and more intimate fellowship with Jesus."
~ Charles H. Spurgeon

My church holds Hope, Healing, and Recovery classes on Tuesday nights. When I started going to this church I remember thinking, "Wow, they have such great praise and worship music. I sure wish they had a mid-week service." I saw in the bulletin that they had this thing on Tuesday nights called H2O, Spiritual Growth & Recovery.

From its description it looked like it was for people with "issues" and I didn't have any issues (or so I thought). In fact at the time I first became aware of the class, my life was going really well — I had just moved to San Antonio, I had started dating a guy, who I knew was "the one," and I had bought a house — all my goals and dreams were coming true. I kind of felt bad for people who had all those problems. Here I was two years later, and now I was one of those people.

The first night of the class happened to be the same day that I had spoken with my ex-husband whom I hadn't spoken with in over five years. The conversation with my ex-husband had brought up so many emotions and suppressed memories, that I just sat in a chair and cried the whole time as people were sharing their testimonies and we were being oriented to the class.

Celebrate Recovery[11] is a biblically based 12 step recovery program based on the beatitudes. I was in a small group of about 10 people, whom I met with weekly for 9 months. During that time we would work through the principles based on the beatitudes and answer the questions as it applied to each of us as individuals. We were not allowed to talk with or try to fix other people. We were there to work on ourselves and allow God to work within us. Each week, we would go around the group verbalizing our answers to the questions. Each person would actively listen to and acknowledge the person who was speaking without judgment, without blame, and without speaking. It was a safe place to be and an incredible process to work through.

The first step in the journey through recovery is getting out of denial. I had been in denial for so long — denial that my ex-boyfriend and I were not going to get back together and that he had chosen not to be with me and denial that I was experiencing depression and that I needed help. I had resisted this because I didn't want the stigma of being depressed. I remember when I called to make appointments to be seen, I didn't even want to use the word depression.

When the appointment clerk asked what my appointment was for, I would say it was to follow up on allergies, which was not untrue, but it was not my primary reason for being seen. I wanted to be tough, to just suck it up, and move on like I had done with my marriage. My ego did not want to admit that I was sick, that I needed help, and that I couldn't handle it by myself.

Once I took the step of ownership for where I was, how I was feeling, and the choices that had gotten me to where I was, then I had the freedom to choose something different. I was able to release my illusion of control, own my powerlessness, and step into God's freedom and grace. That's all that God wanted all along — for me to release my life to Him and trust Him. But I didn't want to release. Just like Jacob, I had many late nights of wrestling with God. Why was He doing what He was doing? From my small, finite perspective it didn't make any sense. And God has a much bigger perspective than me and a much *bigger* and better plan for me than I had for myself.

"My thoughts are nothing like your thoughts," says the Lord. "And my ways are far beyond anything you could imagine. For just as the heavens are higher than the earth, so my ways are higher than your ways and my thoughts higher than your thoughts." ~ Isaiah 55:8-9 NLT

Through this process I was able to finally release. "God, I am tired, I am tired of doing everything on my own strength. I am tired of crying and being sad. I am tired of being tired. I am done. My whole life I have done things on my own strength and look where it has gotten me. I am tired of living in struggle. I choose to release; to give it all to you. You said in the Bible to cast all of our cares on you. If your Word is the Truth, then I have nothing to lose and everything to gain. What I've been doing isn't working, so I'm trying something new. I'm giving my life over to you. Let's see if what you say is really true."

"Come to me, all you who are weary and burdened, and I will give you rest. Take my yoke upon you and learn from me, for I am gentle and humble in heart, and you will find rest for your souls. For my yoke is easy and my burden is light." ~ Matthew 11:28-30 NIV

What a release I felt! I don't have to have the world on my shoulders anymore. I don't have to fix everything and everyone. That is God's job, not mine. My whole life I have been trying to play god with myself and with others. That's not my job; no wonder it was so exhausting! So what God really wants, is for me to just release everything to Him, let Him be in charge, and trust Him completely?

Hmm...sounds too good to be true. But what if it's not? What if what God wants, more than anything, is for me to trust Him and be in relationship with Him — to trust Him with everything?

A critical part of the recovery process was doing a personal inventory — creating an inventory of everyone whom I have hurt and everyone who has hurt me. It felt yucky and painful drudging up that stuff. I tried to forget those things, to push them out of my memory.

Yet, what if I could not be completely healed until I worked through that process? Part of working through that process was for me to own what was mine to own. I had made poor choices in my life. I had made decisions and had done things that had hurt other people. This wasn't about justifying why I did what I did. It was not about deflecting my responsibility by bringing up the other person's faults. This was about owning my part in whatever was done. This was about being real, being raw, and being honest.

As I worked through my inventory, I was able to see trends of belief systems that I held and I became aware of why I act the way I do. Do you remember in chapter one when I mentioned that by the time children were eight years old 80% of their belief systems were already set? Listen to this...

When I was young, I remember having this conversation with my father. He would be in his chair watching TV after waking up at four in the morning and having a long day at

CHAPTER 13 ~ PEELING BACK THE ONION

work. I would say, "Dad, dad, dad, dad, dad, dad." He would be watching TV and would look up after about the sixth "dad" and say, "What, honey?"

The belief system that I had created around that conversation at six years old was that I was not important. Now, was that the truth? No, my dad absolutely loved me and thought that I was important. He was simply tired after a long day at work. Yet, what I had created that to mean was that I was not important, that I couldn't keep guys' attention, and that I wasn't worth paying attention to.

How did that translate to my adult life? Fast forward to my relationship with my ex-husband. When he cheated on me, this reinforced my belief about myself that I was not important, that I was not desirable, that I was not lovable, that I was not enough.

Fast forward to the break-up with my ex-boyfriend, when he cut off communication with me and refused to return phone calls or acknowledge my existence, this reinforced to me that I wasn't important, that I wasn't lovable, that I wasn't desirable, that I wasn't worth being with, that I wasn't enough. I was so small that he didn't even acknowledge my existence.

Those were my truths. They were what I believed about myself. Holding on to those beliefs was what allowed me to spiral down into a severe depression. And those circumstances just reinforced what I believed about myself and allowed me to prove myself right. Wow, right? They weren't conscious choices. They were unconscious belief systems that I had created based on stories that I had made up regarding situations that had occurred.

What if each of us has thousands of unconscious belief systems that were created by stories that we have made up regarding situations that have occurred in our lives? What if 80% of our belief systems were developed by the time that we were eight years old and affected each and every decision we make as an adult?

What if the only way to change these belief systems is to become aware of them? What if once we became aware of them, we could make a choice regarding whether they serve us or not and whether we want to keep them? What if we could change the story we made up regarding certain situations at any time? What if we could choose to create stories that serve us and what we want in life, rather than believe stories that keep us stuck?

Part of the inventory process was to go through the inventory out loud with a sponsor, who had previously been through the Celebrate Recovery program. My sponsor listened to me go through my inventory without judgment, without blame, and with love and compassion. I told her things that I had never told anyone before. It was a freeing process. The best part of the whole process was the very last day that our group got together, we burned our inventory sheets!

"This means that anyone who belongs to Christ has become a new person. The old life is gone; a new life has begun!" ~ 2 Corinthians 5:17 NLT

It was so freeing to own and then let go of that which wasn't serving me. I was able to acknowledge past events in my life, evaluate all my relationships, forgive those who had hurt me, and make amends to those whom I had hurt. There was no more hiding, no more pretending things didn't happen, and no more pretending to have the perfect life. There was just me being honest, being vulnerable, and being humble.

Was it uncomfortable? Yes. Was it worth the freedom that was waiting for me on the other side? Yes!

CHAPTER 14:

A New Mind

"If you are depressed you are living in the past.
If you are anxious you are living in the future.
If you are at peace you are
living in the present."
~ Lao Tzu

Through the Celebrate Recovery class I was able to get connected with a professional counselor who practiced through a Biblical worldview. Through working with her, I was able to identify mindsets that weren't serving me and replace them with the Truth of God's Word.

What had kept me stuck for so long was that when memories came up, I would start to feel sad, I would then focus on more memories and try to figure things out. When I did this, it would take me down a rabbit hole of sadness and despair, where I would keep myself stuck. After starting to work with my counselor, I was able to identify the thoughts and feelings as they started to come on; I would then consciously choose to shift my focus from past memories to God.

Just like the dog in training that I talked about earlier, I would keep my eyes on my master and that would keep me from getting distracted by feelings or circumstances. I would then use the sword of the spirit to speak God's truths over my life.

One of my personal life coaches helped me walk through an exercise where I identified mindsets that weren't serving me. Once I identified what they were, then I was able to create a new story around them.

Mindset that wasn't serving me	New story that I chose to create
My ex-boyfriend was "the one."	God has someone and something BETTER planned for me.
My worth is dependent on my accomplishments.	My worth is based on who I am, not what I do. I am perfect as God is perfect. I am a child of the King.
Money is hard to get.	Money is easy to get. Money flows into my life. God is my provider. He promises that if I bring my tithes into the storehouse He will open the windows of heaven.

I refuse to fail.	I now recognize that this statement is my ego talking. A perceived failure may be a huge win if I lean into my beingness and play full out. It is who I become in the process of the fulfillment of my goal that counts. It's about the journey.
I am not important.	I am significant. I am a child of the King. I am made in the image of God. God has a plan especially designed for me. As I step into that plan, I step into my destiny.
I need to do in order to be productive.	My worth is not defined by what I do, but rather who I am intrinsically. I choose to be all that I am and choose to walk in my beingness as a playful, open, cherished, sensuous, worthy, abundant, significant, peaceful, and joyous woman of God!
I am lazy if I'm not being or doing something productive.	I am showing myself self-love when I honor myself through relaxing and refreshing my soul with things that are enjoyable to me.
I have high expectations of myself and others and I always find myself disappointed.	I have no expectations of myself or others; this allows me to be surprised and delighted instead of constantly disappointed. I am human; others are human. I will always be disappointed when I expect myself and others to be perfect. Only God is perfect. He will never disappoint.

This was a fascinating, yet humbling process. It was like I was playing detective with myself. All of a sudden I became aware of sunglasses (ways of thinking) that I had had my whole life. Once I became aware of them, then I could evaluate whether they served me or not, and whether I wanted to keep them or replace them with ones that did served me.

There were so many lies that I had been telling myself my whole life. I had actually believed them to be true. Until I recognized the lies, I couldn't replace them. What were the lies that I had been telling myself?

1. I can't or don't have loving relationships because:
    I'm a bad judge of character
    I don't know how to love right
    I'm not lovable
    I'm not worth being with or fighting for

2. I don't have enough money because:
    I don't make enough
    I'm not good at finances
    Money bores me
    There is never enough
    I don't save enough
    I don't like keeping track
    My goals are too high
    I have expensive taste
    I don't keep track well enough

3. I don't love myself unconditionally because:
    I'm not perfect
    I make bad choices
    I'm a bad judge of character

I'm not important enough
That's selfish
I make mistakes
I can be lazy

4. I don't have fun because:
    I'm too busy
    It's frivolous
    I don't have time
    It's a waste of time
    I'm not a fun person
    I'm boring
    I choose not to
    It's awkward
    I put myself last and choose productivity first
    I don't know how
    I don't want to (or know how to) by myself
    I'm saving those experiences to do with my future
      husband
    It would mean that I'm not being productive

5. I don't accept God's love for me because:
    I don't deserve it
    I make mistakes
    I'm not perfect
    I make bad choices
    I disappoint Him
    I'm not worth it
    I'm not lovable
    I don't know how

As I spent time listening to what I would say and think, these are the things that I would hear myself saying...

> "I don't want to bother him/her."
> "I don't mean to cause trouble."
> "I'm all about low profile."
> "I'm not that important."
> "I'm bad (I feel guilty) because I'm using money I had set aside for emergencies."
> "It's not that important."

It was interesting listening to myself without having judgment of good, bad, right, or wrong. These sentences are a reflection of what I unconsciously believed to be true.

Were they the truth? No, absolutely not. Yet, I had run my life as though they were. I had believed that they were. I had felt that they were. But that was before I became aware of them. Now that I am aware of them, I can make new choices. I can create new stories-ones that serve me and are based on the Truth of God's Word.

"Do not conform to the pattern of this world, but be transformed by the renewing of your mind. Then you will be able to test and approve what God's will is-his good, pleasing, and perfect will."
~ Romans 12:2 NIV

CHAPTER 15:

Who Am I?

"As self-betrayers we project an image of a deserving, worthwhile person, and then we struggle constantly to produce evidence that we're measuring up to that image. This is hard work and exceedingly stressful... We are neither the ideal people we fancy ourselves to be, nor the worthless kind of persons we sometimes suspect we are."
~ C. Terry Warner

Three years ago if you would have asked me who I was, I would have told you, "I know exactly who I am. I am Bethany Connor, Army Nurse Corps officer." I was a cocky and confident young Army officer who knew exactly what to do, what to say, and what I thought about everything. That was the mask that I wanted everyone to see — my GI Jane façade: "I'm tough." "I can handle it." "I'm in control."

I threw myself into my work. Work was my life. I defined myself by my job position and what I accomplished. I got my sense of self-worth by being admired, being needed, and being validated by others.

I remember a phone conversation with my ex-boyfriend about this very thing. We were talking about my job as an Army Nurse Corps officer and he told me, "It's what you do, it's not who you are." I found that statement to be absolutely profound. What do you mean that it's not who I am? Of course it's who I am.

Or was it? What if my job was merely what I did, but did not define who I was? If that was the case, then I had no idea who I was! I had spent the past 16 years of my Army career defining myself by my rank, my job position, and what I accomplished. I had thrown myself into my work. Work was my life. It was who I was. It defined me. So, if indeed my work as an Army Nurse Corps officer was simply what I did, but wasn't who I was, then who was I?

I had no idea who I was. I had spent my life hiding behind masks — the mask of perfection; the mask of being tough; the mask of being in control; the mask of being right; the mask of being knowledgeable. I wore so many masks, that I did not know who I was. Who was the "real" me? Who was Bethany Connor?

As I started to ask these questions, I found there to be a dichotomy between who I really was and who I wanted to be seen as. I felt as though I was living two lives — there was Bethany Connor, Army Nurse Corps officer, then there was the "real" me. I could not possibly be the "real" me while in uniform. That would be too vulnerable, too risky, too unsafe.

As an officer and a leader in the Army, I was expected to have it all together, to be in control, to exemplify the epitome of military bearing. If indeed there were two sides of me, I would have to keep the "real" me for off-duty. That was my only option. It was what was expected. That was the way it had to be.

Living out of alignment with my authentic self was exhausting! As I began to discover who I really was, who I was did not match who I was trying to be seen as at all. The challenge was to let the two become one. I couldn't possibly do that. I mean, be my authentic self, be the "real" me? I would never be accepted in the military. It wasn't safe. People would judge me. I would get eaten alive. I would never survive!

And what if they rejected the "real" me? Then that would really hurt. At least now, if they reject the person I am pretending to be, it won't really hurt because it's not really me. It's business; it's not personal; that would make it way too personal and I don't want to feel the pain of rejection.

What if I could live a life in alignment though? What if I could be the authentic me no matter where I was or who I was with? How would that feel?

Wow, that would feel really good, actually. It would feel absolutely freeing — to be who I am authentically without apology, without excuse. That would be nice. But again, I'm brought back to the question, "Who am I?" Well, if the Word of God is the Truth, who does God say I am?

> *For you created my inmost being;*
> *you knit me together in my mother's womb.*
> *I praise you because I am fearfully and wonderfully made;*
> *your works are wonderful,*
> *I know that full well.*
> *My frame was not hidden from you*
> *when I was made in the secret place.*
> *When I was woven together in the depths of the earth,*
> *your eyes saw my unformed body.*
> *All the days ordained for me*
> *were written in your book*
> *before one of them came to be.* ~ Psalm 139:14-16 NIV

What if it were true that I am fearfully and wonderfully made? What if God truly knit me together and created me uniquely for His divine purpose? What if God knew me so intimately that he knows the number of hairs on my head?

"Are not five sparrows sold for two pennies? Yet, not one of them is forgotten by God. Indeed, the very hairs of your head are all numbered. Don't be afraid; you are worth more than many sparrows." ~ Luke 12:6-7 NIV

Wow, He knows the number of hairs on my head! He wrote every day of my life before I was even born? That makes me feel pretty significant, pretty important, pretty loved!

That's nothing though, get this: I was made in the image of God!

"So God created human beings in his own image. In the image of God he created them; male and female he created them." ~ Genesis 1:27 NLT

Okay, wait a minute. If I, Bethany Connor, was made in the image of God, what does that mean? That would mean that I have *all* the characteristics of God. So back when I asked the facilitator, "What if you don't want certain qualities?"

And the facilitator responded, "It doesn't have to be either/or, you can have it all."

She was right! Not only can I have certain qualities, I *do* have certain qualities! I have all the qualities of God innately within me. All I have to do is choose to step into those qualities. They are already a part of who I am!

Well, if that's the case and I already have all the qualities of God, then I don't need to pretend anything. I am whole and complete just as I am. I am whole and complete in Him.

"For in Christ lives all the fullness of God in a human body. So you also are complete through your union with Christ, who is the head over every ruler and authority." ~ Colossians 2:9-10 NLT

How empowering! How freeing! To know that I AM everything that I always thought that I wasn't. I am now free to be me — free to be who I was created to be! I am free to live in authentic confidence of who I am and the value that I have to share with the world. I am no longer defined by my circumstances or my accomplishments. I am defined by the One who created me!

CHAPTER 16:

Just BE

"The thing that is really hard, and really amazing is giving up on being perfect and beginning the work of becoming yourself."
~ Anna Quindlen

I think I had to come to the end of *trying* to do it all myself and trying to fix circumstances that were beyond my realm of control, to finally be willing to look internally. I did not have control over the situations in my life, but I *did* have control over how I responded to those situations. I also learned to stop *trying* to do things on my own strength and to trust that God has a bigger plan and has all things under His control.

It's amazing how tiring trying can be. My mentor, Patrick Dean has an amazing way to demonstrate the futility of trying. Do this: stand up from sitting in a chair. Okay, now try to sit down. No, no, don't *sit* down, just *try* to sit down. Trying can be very tiring and takes so much more effort than just doing.[12]

One morning as I was sitting on the edge of my pool, God began to speak with me,

> "Bethany, it's not what you do, it's who you are. Stop focusing on doing and start focusing on *being*. Just be. Stop trying and just be. You will not be able to do it on your own strength. Choose to just *be* and let me *do* through you. That is the answer. You will not be able to figure out how on your own strength. The how is through me — through my grace and empowerment. Stop *trying* to change. Stop *trying* to be. Just *be*.
>
> Remember the trying exercise with Patrick. You're making this way harder than it has to be by trying. You already have the answer within you. Be who you are. Who you are is enough. I have made you, perfectly. Believe that. Believe in me. Do not listen to the lies of the devil. Do not listen to the lies of the world. They will try to deceive you. Trust in me. Follow in obedience. Rely on my Word. My Word is the Truth. It is your guide and it will lead you along the path."

Then I looked down to the pool. I saw leaves floating. I saw a bug struggling in the water, until it bumped into a leaf. It then struggled to get out of the water and onto the leaf. Once it got on the leaf, it was safe; however, it kept moving and ended up falling back into the water. Again it struggled, first to move from its back to its front, and then struggled in the water. Finally it came to a leaf again, it struggled to get onto the leaf where it would be safe and be able to survive, but it kept moving, working, trying, got to the edge of the leaf, and fell into the water again. I watched this process quite a few times. If the bug had only stopped moving, it would have been safe. I could have picked the bug up and taken it out of the water, but inevitably it would have continued moving and gone back into the water again.

God then spoke to me,

> "Bethany, just like that bug you keep on doing. When you keep on doing you are making more work for yourself. You need to stop doing and start being. Right now you are exhausted. You do not know how to get it all done, so you keep trying harder and harder. Trying is not the answer. The more you try, the more exhausted you will become. You are trying on your own strength. You are doing on your own strength. Stop doing and just be. You be and let Me do through you. Stop trying."

I responded, "But God, I don't know how to be. I don't even know who I really am."

> "Do or do not. There is no try." ~ Yoda

I worked and worked harder and harder to the point that my work was all I knew. My work was how I found my identity. When my ex-boyfriend told me, "It's what you do, it's not who you are," that was a revelation to me. Really? Who I am is enough? But who am I? I don't even know and I don't know how to just be.

All my life I've been a doer. I'm good at doing. That is what I know. I *do* so I don't have to *be*. So I don't have to be lonely, vulnerable, caring, compassionate, or sexy. I don't know how to be the authentic me. That person is a stranger to me and I don't think that I like that person.

I would rather "be seen as" then truly be. Because truly being requires vulnerability; it requires trust. That is not safe. That would allow me to get hurt again and I don't want to get hurt. So I keep doing and doing, to keep myself numb; to keep myself protected; to keep myself safe; to keep myself from getting hurt again.

As I sat on the stairs by the pool, I practiced being. I took a deep breath in, then exhaled. As I was doing that, I brought my hands up to my chest, and then moved them downward as I exhaled out. I did that a couple times to ground and center myself in the Holy Spirit.

Wow, so this is just being? It seemed too easy. I was used to the struggle. This was uncomfortable. How would I get everything done that needs to get done if I was in such a state of peace and contentment? I must go back to busy. I must go back to doing.

But the Holy Spirit spoke to me yet again, "Stop doing and just be. Just *be* and let me *do* through you."

I had heard that before. I knew it intellectually. Knowing in my head and living it out are two different things. That was part of the struggle. But the struggle, the process, was what was most important. I must go through the struggle in order to become the beautiful creation that God intended me to be.

I was a doer. Historically, I had defined myself by what I accomplished. My self-esteem and knowing that I was good enough, came from what I did. When I accomplished things I heard words of affirmation from others and then I felt like I was enough. When I didn't hear words of affirmation, there was a void, so I tried to fill that void by doing so that I could feel like I was enough.

When I accomplished things, then people acknowledged me, praised me, and thought highly of me. They helped to fill that void inside for a split second. And I felt good (about myself and happy with life) for a split second, but it was never enough. That void inside was never filled. It was an insatiable need for acceptance, acknowledgement, and affirmation from others.

When I didn't get it filled then I told myself lies:

~ I'm not enough
~ I'm not lovable
~ I'm not worthy
~ I'll never be happy
~ I'll never be good enough
~ I'll always be alone in life
~ I'm not worth loving
~ I'm not beautiful

These statements are ALL untruths — lies of the devil. I had been going through life counting my worth by what other people thought of me. My life had been driven by the need to:

~ look good
~ be accepted
~ be admired
~ be loved by others
~ feel important
~ be right

I had spent my life doing, doing, doing. The more I did, the more productive I was and that is where I derived my self-worth. I wanted to *do*, to keep busy and be productive so I didn't have to *be*. That's where I was comfortable; that's where I could hide and avoid working on my own stuff.

If I kept busy doing then I wouldn't have to look at myself, who I really was, what I truly desired, because that would be too scary. It would hurt too much. It would be too painful. It would be too vulnerable. What if I could be the most productive and have the biggest impact through being instead of through doing?

What if me doing, kept me from being the best leader that I could be? What if instead of doing it all, to ensure that everything was done perfectly, I empowered others to do? What if I trusted that I didn't have to be in charge; that I didn't have to know everything that was going on? What if things would get done and everything would turn out just as it was supposed to without me knowing, coordinating, and having visibility of everything? What if I could trust that the people I worked with would do what needed to be done.

What if things didn't need to look a certain way, with me at the center of the universe? What if I was not the center of the universe? What if life did not revolve around me? What if things could go smoothly and could get executed without me having to micromanage, to be in control, to be in charge of and what if they didn't have to look a certain way?

What if there were an infinite number of mechanisms for how things could be accomplished? What if it didn't have to look like I thought it had to look? In fact, what if by setting expectations of how things "should" look, I limit God's miraculous greatness and stifle creativity?

What if God's ways are higher than my ways? What if He can do infinitely above anything I hope or dream?[13] If that were the case, then why would I limit Him to my paradigm? What if by doing so, I am missing out on life and all the greatness He has in store for me?

What if I said that I want God's plan for my life, yet I limited Him by setting my expectations of how I thought things should look? And what if when they didn't look how I thought they should look, I got sad, disappointed, and filled with despair?

Seriously? The God of the universe put desires in my heart. He promised me — gave me His unbreakable Word that they would come to pass and because circumstances didn't look the way I thought they should look, I thought that they were not going to happen?

Hello!?! He is the God of the Universe, Maker of ALL things! He knows how many hairs are on my head and I wasn't going to trust Him!?! He promised me, He promised. He does not lie. His promises are true. He LOVES me and wants the best for me. And I didn't trust Him — the Creator of the Universe? Really!?! I think that little, tiny me knows better than the God of the universe!?!

Okay, let's get real now. Not realistic. I said I was a follower of Christ — yet I didn't trust God and His promises to me? I said I believed Him; I said that I had faith and yet when my circumstances didn't look the way I thought they should look, I got sad and depressed?

What if circumstances were just a distraction? God's Word is the Truth. He does not lie and cannot lie because of who He is. His character does not change. Who He is does not change. His Words are true, they transcend time and they transcend circumstances.

I said that I trusted Him, however, my actions up until now had not shown that. I *tried* to act in my own strength. I am now ready to stop trying — to stop doing and to start *being*. Being who I am and stepping into my greatness. I choose to accept *all* of me; all of my imperfections; all of my greatness; all of my hearts desires; the good, the bad, and the humanity.

What if it is okay not to be perfect? What if it is okay to screw up? What if it is okay to embrace my humanity and choose to live daily in the grace of God? What if I can screw up, make mistakes, not be perfect, and accept the love and forgiveness of my perfect unchanging Heavenly Father? How cool would that be?

What if I could trust the Creator of the Universe with my life, with my future, with my heart's desires (that He placed there)? What if until I accept "what is," not just how things currently are or seem to be in life, but also who I am fully and completely — the good, the bad, the imperfections, the humanity — will I not be able to move into "what will be?" I'm tired of being stuck. I'm tired of living in insanity-doing the same things over and over, relying on my own strength and expecting things to be different.

What if God will let me be stuck? What if He will let me keep walking around the desert for forty years trying to do my own thing? I could do that, which would be just prolonging it; it would be just wasted time. What if God will let me run around in circles, chasing my own tail, as long as I choose to do that? And what if, when I got tired enough of doing things on my own strength, I could choose to finally let go — to let go of what I think things should look like, to release what is, as well as my hopes, dreams, and desires to Him?

And what if I could choose to *trust* Him completely — not holding back, not taking things back — *completely*!?!. What if I chose to trust the God of the Universe with my life? (Yes, He can handle it.) What if I choose to trust God with my future? What if I choose to trust God with my hopes, dreams, and heart's desires? And what if He will not fail me?

Wow. How refreshing! How relaxing! So, I didn't have to live in struggle? I didn't have to live in despair? I didn't have to live in mistrust? I didn't have to live a life of running around in circles, doing, doing, doing, trying to fill a void — an insatiable void, a God-sized void?

What if it is a God-sized void? What if He could fill that void? What if I were complete in Him? What if nothing and no one else could fill that void, no one but Him — the Creator of the Universe? What if nothing and no one could fill that God-sized void except for Him?

What if I didn't have to try to impress people? What if I was confident enough in myself and who I am that I was content to just be me? What if it didn't matter what people thought of me? What if I didn't need people to like me or to be impressed with me? What if I were enough just as I was?

What if stepping into being enough allowed me the freedom to *be* who I am without apology, without an agenda, without looking for validation by others? What if the only validation I really need is being validated by God? What if I was free to *be* me!?!

CHAPTER 17:

I Am NOT Codependent

"God, grant me the serenity
to accept the things I cannot change,
The courage to change the things I can,
And the wisdom to know the difference."
~ Reinhold Niebuhr

As I started working with my counselor, one of the first books that she recommend that I read was, *Codependent No More* by Melody Beattie.[14] I felt highly offended by this suggestion. I had no idea what codependency was, but whatever it was, it did not describe me! I was not co-dependent and I read the book just to prove it to her!

As I read the book, it went over characteristics of people who were codependent. There were 10 pages of characteristics. The ones listed below are the ones that I personally identified with.

~ feel compelled to help people solve problems and offer unwanted advice
~ anticipate other people's needs
~ wonder why others don't do the same for them
~ find themselves saying "yes" when they mean "no"
~ tell themselves what they want or need is not important
~ feel safest when giving
~ feel insecure and guilty when somebody gives to them
~ over commit themselves
~ feel angry and unappreciated
~ get angry, defensive, self-righteous, and indignant when others blame and criticize them, even though that is something that they do regularly to themselves
~ reject compliments or praise
~ get depressed from a lack of compliments and praise
~ feel guilty about spending money on themselves or doing unnecessary or fun things for themselves
~ take things personally
~ are afraid of making mistakes
~ expect themselves to do everything perfectly
~ have a lot of "shoulds"
~ feel a lot of guilt

~ get artificial feelings of self-worth from helping others
~ wish other people would like and love them
~ become afraid to let themselves be who they are
~ become afraid to let other people be who they are
  and allow events to happen naturally
~ don't see or deal with their fear of loss of control
~ think they know best how things should turn out and
  how people should behave
~ try to control events and people through advice-
  giving or domination
~ get frustrated and angry
~ feel controlled by events or people
~ ignore problems or pretend they aren't happening
~ pretend circumstances aren't as bad as they are
~ stay busy so they don't have to think about things
~ feel depressed
~ become workaholics
~ often seek love from people incapable of loving
~ don't take time to see if other people are good for
  them
~ lose interest in their own lives when they love
~ wonder if they will ever find love
~ advise
~ gauge their words carefully to achieve a desired effect
~ try to say what they think will please people
~ try to say what they hope will make people do what
  they want them to do
~ talk too much
~ avoid talking about themselves, their problems, feelings, and thoughts

- ~ have a difficult time expressing their emotions honestly, openly, and appropriately
- ~ apologize for bothering people
- ~ say they won't tolerate certain behaviors from other people
- ~ gradually increase their tolerance until they can tolerate and do things they said they never would
- ~ let others hurt them
- ~ keep letting people hurt them
- ~ wonder why they hurt so badly
- ~ complain, blame, and try to control while they continue to stand there
- ~ don't trust their feelings
- ~ don't trust their decisions
- ~ don't trust other people
- ~ feel very scared, hurt, and angry
- ~ feel increasing amounts of anger, resentment, and bitterness
- ~ feel safer with their anger than with hurt feelings
- ~ become martyrs, sacrificing their happiness and that of others for causes that don't require sacrifice
- ~ find it difficult to have fun and be spontaneous
- ~ don't seek help because they tell themselves the problem isn't bad enough or they aren't important enough[15]

Okay, maybe I did have a few codependent tendencies. But I didn't like being labeled. So, what now? If I was codependent, how could I fix myself? As my pastor John Witte would say, "You need to name it to tame it." Just like with the recovery process, the first step was getting out of denial. Once I became aware of it, then I had choice around how I wanted to address it.

Trying to fix everyone else — I used to think that was a gift. Now I see that it was me being co-dependent. Even as I was reading the book, I was thinking of all the people who needed to read that book. There I went deflecting attention away from me, wanting to play god and be the savior for everyone else.

What if me trying to "fix" other people, was my way of not dealing with my own stuff? What if I simply accepted people where they were and loved them right where they were? What if I allowed others to walk their own journey, make their own discoveries about themselves, and I focused working on my own stuff?

Wouldn't that be selfish just focusing on me? What if the best way for me to truly help others was to role model the process by working on myself? What if through my own self-discovery process people would notice changes, become curious, and would come to me to learn more?

What if I didn't have to push my agenda on people or what I think things should look like? What if I were detached from the outcome and allowed whatever was supposed to happen to happen? What if I trusted God? What if I trusted myself? What if I trusted the process?

What if I set healthy boundaries that let in the good while keeping out the bad? What if I recognized my feelings, owned them, and then let them go? What if I didn't need to let my feelings dictate my actions? What if I didn't have judgments against my feelings (i.e., I shouldn't feel this way)? What if I noticed my feelings, acknowledged them, and then chose to release them? How would that feel?

I have always been a perfectionist. I like to do everything with excellence because it is a reflection of me. I expected myself to be perfect. When I would accomplish things, instead of focusing on what I did right, I would always focus in on the one area that wasn't perfect or that I could have done better.

I am an encourager and always love to encourage and support other people, but when it comes to myself, I am critical and judgmental. When I started listening to myself, I realized how mean I was to myself. I would not tolerate other people talking to me the way that I talk to myself — not out loud mind you, it was internal self-talk.

Wow! What a powerful thing to notice about myself.

What if I didn't have to be perfect? What if I could be perfectly imperfect just the way I am? What if I gave myself grace; grace to make mistakes, to not be perfect? What if I accepted God's grace? He doesn't expect me to be perfect. He knows that I am human and He loves me just the way I am, mistakes and all.

He loves me so much that He doesn't want me to stay the way I am. He wants me to walk into the incredible destiny and future that He has planned for me. He wants me to accept His love, His forgiveness, and His grace as a gift. There is nothing I have to do to earn His free gift. All I have to do is ask Him for it and receive it. He wants to lavish me with His love and favor! He wants me to be perfect just as He is perfect!

"God saved you by his grace when you believed. And you can't take credit for this; it is a gift from God. Salvation is not a reward for the good things we have done, so none of us can boast about it For we are God's masterpiece. He has created us anew in Christ Jesus, so we can do the good things he planned for us long ago." ~ Ephesians 2:8-10 NLT

CHAPTER 18:

Healthy Boundaries

Boundaries, now that was a foreign concept to me. I did not know that I didn't have boundaries until I became aware of it through the self-discovery process.

I grew up in a small town where everyone knew everyone. My family was very close — my immediate family and my extended family. Most of my uncles, cousins, and grandparents lived within a three-mile radius of my house.

Back in those days we didn't lock the doors to our houses, we left the keys in our cars in the driveway, and our houses were always open. Family and friends would come over and walk in the house without knocking or come over to swim or work in the garage without coordinating ahead of time. That was the way it was. We were an open and loving family. If someone knocked before entering, or called to ask permission to use the pool, that would be considered strange. That was not the culture in my family.

As a child, if my mom was making something for dinner that I didn't want, I would call down to my Grandmother's house to find out what she was having. If I liked her dinner better, I would just tell my mom I was going over to eat at my Grandmother's house. I would get on my bike and ride down to Grandma's for dinner. Grandma always cooked enough for extra guests because she never knew when any of her children or grandchildren might drop by for dinner.

My cousins and I would take trips up to the local dairy farm and play in the barn with the stray cats after school. Before we left, we would each get a container of coffee milk and just write it on my Grandmother's tab. She didn't mind. That was okay in our family.

Our family always stuck together and helped one another out. If someone had a need, we would all pitch in and help that person out. It was expected. My grandmother is such a caring and generous woman that she would give the shirt off her back if anyone in our family was in need. We are family. We protect one another, we support one another, and we love one another. I love all those things about my family!

The second book that my counselor recommended that I read was the book *Boundaries: When to Say Yes How to Say No To Take Control of Your Life* by Dr. Henry Cloud and Dr. John Townsend[16]. Since she was right about the first book, I didn't bother arguing with her this time. I didn't quite understand what boundaries were, but I was open to learning about them.

As I learned about the concept of boundaries, I came to understand that boundaries are not walls; they are like a fence with a gate. The fence is surrounding me and I can choose to open the gate to let in that which serves me and close the gate to keep out what does not serve me.

I have choice in regards to what I choose to let in and what I choose not to let in. I do not "have" to do things out of "guilt" or "obligation." I have choice over what I choose to do and what I choose not to do. Fascinating. I did a lot of things out of guilt and obligation. To say no to someone without having a good reason — I'm allowed to do that?

My church offered a series on boundaries and gave the following guiding principles:

~ Boundaries are to protect me. They are invisible fences. They are necessary for me to learn how to be a friend to myself.
~ I am responsible to know, guard, and communicate my boundaries and limits.
~ As I learn to set my boundaries, I learn to respect other people's boundaries.
~ Internal boundaries are essential so that we don't blame others for our emotions.
~ External boundaries define who and what we allow into our physical space.[17]

Knowing my boundaries clearly defines what *is* my responsibility and what is not my responsibility. I am *not* responsible for other people's happiness, behavior, choices, or feelings. I *am* responsible for my own happiness, behavior, choices, and feelings.

If someone else makes a bad choice or chooses to get angry that is not my responsibility? No. I don't have to fix someone else or try to make someone else happy? No. Each person is responsible for his or her own happiness.

If someone makes a bad choice, I don't need to feel embarrassed, try to fix what happened, or try to protect that person from the consequence of their action? No. In fact, if I protect someone from experiencing the consequence of his/her actions that is called enabling and that is a codependent behavior. That does not help the other person; in fact it keeps that person from growing up and taking responsibility for himself/herself.

Wow, that was a new concept for me to learn.

I remember when my brother got married and moved into the house that we grew up in. He started locking the doors to the house! What the heck? That wasn't how we did things in our family! Why in the world was he locking the house? I felt a bit offended and put off. As I started to learn about boundaries, I learned that people who don't have boundaries often times feel offended when others set their own boundaries. That was true for me. I didn't understand why my brother would do that. That wasn't what we had learned growing up.

As I learned more about this concept, I realized that I did not have any boundaries when it came to work. As far as I was concerned, I was an officer twenty-four hours a day, seven days a week. I was on duty at all times and I could be called in at any time.

I carried a pager with me and my staff knew that I was always available if they needed anything at all. I worked long hours because the staff "needed" me. Did they really need me? No. In fact, it would have supported them more for me to empower them to make decisions on their own and grow as nurses and as leaders.

Instead, I coddled them by being available anytime; nights, weekends, after hours. They knew they could count on me. I was secretly jealous of people who left promptly at 4:00 p.m. to go to the gym or to pick up their kids. I was more dedicated than they were I told myself. The truth was that they had boundaries and I did not. They role modeled balance in their lives. I was role modeling imbalance and lack of boundaries. The more that I learned about boundaries, the more that I learned that I didn't have them!

The cool thing was, now that I was aware of boundaries, I could start practicing setting healthy boundaries. What would healthy boundaries look like in my life?

~ Setting a specific time to exercise and stick to that time no matter what.
~ To say "no" when I did not want to do something, without having to justify or come up with an excuse.
~ Not letting people borrow money out of a sense of obligation, especially when I had specific plans on how I was going to use that money.
~ Setting boundaries with myself on how long I spent on the computer each night.

~ Choosing to step away when I was with people who were gossiping or talking bad about someone else, instead of getting pulled into the drama.

~ Being honest about what I truly wanted to do and didn't want to do.

~ Choosing to surround myself with positive people who will challenge me and support me with growing forward in life.

~ Having open, honest, responsible communication with people.

~ Identifying and being aware of my true feelings and intentionally choosing if, when, and how I will communicate my feelings.

Wow! Just writing those things feels empowering. I am only responsible for myself, not for other people. I choose not to let other people's emotions or life circumstances define how I feel or the choices that I make. I choose when to say "yes" and when to say "no" and whatever I choose is okay.

CHAPTER 19:

Learning to Love Myself

In January of 2012, I started the highest level of leadership training currently offered through Brian Klemmer's leadership and character development company[18]. It was a four month long intense program that involved weekly master-mind calls with a small group and coach and two experiential weekend seminars. This training was the most challenging leadership training that I have experienced in my life thus far.

Each of the individual participants had to identify and achieve both a personal goal and a professional goal. This was easy I thought; I am totally good at achieving goals. When I set my mind to something, I achieve it.

Before I arrived at my first weekend of training, we got together with our small groups to refine our goals, I already had some ideas in my mind. For the professional goal, maybe I would max my Army physical training test or do a triathlon, those are things I hadn't done before and I could accomplish in a ten-week period.

For my personal goal I thought I might do something around dating. While staffing a leadership workshop right before the four month training began, I had a revelation that I had been keeping myself busy with things that didn't really matter to me, while neglecting the one thing that I really wanted more than anything — to be in an intimately fulfilling, fun, loving, wholesome, and committed relationship with the man of my dreams. I had kept so busy accomplishing goals that weren't really important to me, while keeping myself from pursuing the one thing that I wanted most. That was a big "aha" for me.

The goals that we came up with had to be S.M.A.R.T. goals— **S**pecific, **M**easurable, **A**ttainable, **R**isky, and have a specific **T**ime frame.

Our mastermind teams helped us to refine our goals and had to be in agreement with our goals. These were not easy, sissy goals. These were risky, "oh my gosh, what in the world am I doing, this is so outside of my comfort zone" goals. By the time my goals were finalized, I had those types of goals.

My professional goal was: On or before May 4, 2012 I will earn $2,000 or more through life coaching clients.

That goal looked nothing like what I had been thinking of and boy was it uncomfortable. About six months prior to this training, I had started taking classes to become a

Certified Life Coach. I had initially signed up for the class because I wanted to learn to ask better questions.

I did a lot of coaching, teaching, and mentoring in my position as an Army officer. It was easy for me to tell people what to do and use my rank to make it happen. However, my experience with that type of leadership is that it results in compliance and not commitment. I wanted to learn to ask better questions, so that the people that I worked with could come up with the answers for themselves. I wanted to empower them to be part of the solution and create commitment to what needed to be done, rather than compliance.

As I moved forward with the life coaching classes, I had the opportunity to work with peer coaches and coach mentors. The coaching skills that I developed were such an amazing gift! The sessions that I had with other coaches really helped me to develop life skills that have moved me forward exponentially in discovering my true self and stepping into that person on a daily basis.

Not only did I develop skills that will serve me well in my role as an Army officer; I developed skills that are serving me well in life! These skills have improved my relationships with my family and friends — taking them to a whole other level. They have also empowered me to approach both my business and personal interactions from openness and curiosity rather than judgment.

As I finished up my coaching class, the instructors talked about developing a coaching niche — a specialty area of focus. I wasn't sure what my niche would be — probably leadership and healthcare. That was where a majority of my life experience was. Luckily, I had only joined the coaching class for my edification, so I wouldn't have to worry about figuring out a coaching niche. I figured it might be something I could do for fun after I retired from the military, but had no intentions of doing anything with it right then, other than using it in my daily life.

As my mastermind team and I worked on what my goals looked like, they started asking me about areas of interest. I told them about the life coaching class that I was taking. My eyes lit up as I was telling them about it and the passion of all that I was learning just exuded from me.

That's when my team told me I should do a goal around life coaching. Hmmm, I hadn't even considered that. Well, I guess I could do my goal around life coaching. Yeah, I'll say that I'll need to get a certain number of clients over the ten-week period, I could do that. I told my team that I thought that was doable.

They challenged me, "Oh no, you are not doing it around a number of clients, you are doing it around earning money." Earning money? You mean charge people for coaching them? That was totally a foreign concept to me and very uncomfortable. I coach and mentor people all the time in the Army and I don't charge people. I had a lot of stuff come up around me charging for my coaching services; I wasn't that important; If people needed my help, I always helped them; I was a "new" coach…

My team reminded me that I was a Lieutenant Colonel in the Army with sixteen years of experience in leadership, coaching, and mentoring. I also was a Clinical Nurse

Specialist in Adult Health in Geriatrics with sixteen years of nursing experience.

By that time I had completed my coaching class. I had attended all of the leadership and character development classes offered through Brian's company. I had been taking transformational leadership and workshop facilitation classes through another company and had even voluntarily staffed additional classes to increase my knowledge and experience. I had completed Celebrate Recovery and was a leader and sponsor for others going through the class. I had been working with a Christian Counselor for a year. Okay, well, maybe I did have something to offer as a life coach that was worth charging money for.

My personal goal was: On or before May 4, 2012 I would complete *The Love Dare* book[19] on myself.

I had a fascinating revelation during my first weekend training event, when I realized that I didn't love myself! All these years, I thought I had loved myself. I had acted confident in who I was, but deep down inside, I didn't love myself.

If I had loved myself then I would not have given my power away to someone else. If I had loved myself, then I would not have let someone else's actions or opinions affect how I felt and how I behaved. If I had loved myself, then I would have stood strong in the authentic confidence of who I was and the value I had to offer the world. That was an incredible discovery for me! How could I possibly be loved by anyone else, if I did not love myself?

My team recognized this in me and challenged me to take on learning to love myself. God had handpicked my team, by the way. There were six of us on the team; four guys and two girls, and I'll tell you what, that was the exact team that I needed to be with. Those guys saw in me what I didn't see (or feel) in myself. They loved me, encouraged me, and gave me tough love, all when I needed it.

Going through a book seemed like an easy enough goal, but it was the most challenging goal that I had ever set out to achieve. *The Love Dare* is a book from the movie, Fireproof[20]. In the movie, the husband and wife are having a rough time in their marriage and are at the breaking point of getting a divorce. The husband's father requests his son to read through and do the Love Dare on his wife prior to seeking a divorce. *The Love Dare* is a forty day journey of self-reflection with daily action steps for him to take in his relationship with his wife. Instead of me working through the self-reflection and daily action steps on someone else, I was doing those action steps on myself.

It felt uncomfortable taking the time to do special things for me. And, I chose to push through the discomfort and to honor myself through the process. One day there was a challenge to "buy yourself something that says, 'I was thinking of you today.'" It was 10:30 p.m. and I had yet to do anything for myself. Instead of pushing it off, dismissing it as "not important" and me as "not important," I got in my car and drove to a 24-hour Wal-Mart to buy myself flowers.

While I was in the store, the voice in my head was telling me, "Don't waste money. Buy something practical." While I was looking at which flowers to buy, I decided to buy myself roses — red roses because I'm worth it! I put them in a vase on the desk in my bedroom. It felt honoring to give myself flowers. I felt happy, lovely, deserving, and thankful. It also felt empowering choosing not to listen to the little voice in my head. I was re-writing my old stories and ways of thinking that hadn't served me. I was instead writing new stories that did serve me and empower me to step into the greatness of who I am!

One day I chose to honor myself by going running first thing when I got home from work, and by folding the laundry and putting it away before going to bed. It felt nice to honor myself by running. I always feel better when I honor my body by eating right and exercising. I used to put everything else that I needed to do higher on the priority list and put myself last. When I do that, it perpetuates me not feeling good about myself and thinking and saying mean things to myself that are not true and do not serve me (ex. that I'm lazy for not running).

Now, when I hear myself saying critical or judgmental things about myself — I choose to not accept those thoughts and replace them with something positive and true that will serve me.

"Finally, brothers, whatever is true, whatever is noble, whatever is right, whatever is pure, whatever is lovely, whatever is admirable ~ if anything is excellent or praiseworthy ~ think about such things." Phil 4:8 NIV

One of my biggest cheerleaders on this journey was my friend Ruby. Ruby had been through all of the training previously, so she was an amazing support, especially on the days when I wasn't sure if I'd ever be able to meet my goals. Ruby is also a photographer. In support of both of my goals, Ruby and I coordinated a photo shoot.

Prior to the photo shoot, I went to one of her make-up artists to get made over. When he had finished, I looked in the mirror and did not recognize myself. As far as I could tell, I felt like I had way too much make-up on. I could not remember the last time I wore eye shadow and mascara and never in my life have I ever worn fake eyelashes! It felt very uncomfortable.

At the photo shoot itself, at first I felt self-conscious and weird. Who was I to be getting a photo shoot? I certainly didn't feel pretty. Ruby has a magic way of connecting with people and getting them out of their shell. She certainly did that with me. She allowed me to step into the characteristics that I felt I wasn't, and truly captured my essence on camera. By the end of the photo shoot I was a playful, open, cherished, and sensuous woman!

When she sent me some of the photos the next morning, my eyes started to tear up as I looked at the pictures. "Wow," I thought, "I am kinda pretty."

As I moved forward in achieving my two goals, there was one thing I was doing differently, I was intentionally not achieving the goals on my own strength. All my life, I had accomplished things on my own strength. This time, I wanted it to be different.

This time I was choosing to give the goals to God and let Him accomplish them through me.

It was a constant challenge not to go back to my default of doing and instead release the outcome to God. Certainly I would move forward into action, but the difference this time was that I was following His lead and not my own. It was uncomfortable and scary, and honestly I wasn't sure if He would come through for me. It was a continuous practice of learning to trust in Him on a moment-by-moment basis.

As I pursued the life-coaching goal, I was amazed at how effortlessly and smoothly everything evolved. God revealed to me my coaching niche: Hope for the hurting heart. I just chuckled when He revealed that to me. He really doesn't waste a thing. He was going to use my last two years of struggle through depression, so that I could help other people who were going through that same process. He even gave me a name for my coaching business, Hope 4 the Heart Life Coaching.

"He comforts us in all our troubles so that we can comfort others. When they are troubled, we will be able to give them the same comfort God has given us." ~ 2 Corinthians 1:4 NLT

Now to create the $2,000 in God's strength. One of my personal life coaches got me connected with a graphic designer who created a logo for my website. I had business cards made. One of my girlfriends, who is also a life coach, got me connected with the woman who created her website. She got my website up and going exactly as I had envisioned it. I started working with a Marketing and Branding Coach to help me come up with a marketing plan to accomplish this goal. I came up with a price structure for my coaching business to offer 1:1 coaching. I also put together a 7-week group coaching class. I contacted local organizations and offered my speaking and coaching services. By the 9th week, I had created $1200 worth of income. $800 more to go for me to achieve my goal.

Part of that time, I chose to be in struggle. There were some days when I didn't know if I would achieve my goal or not. At any time, I could have chosen to do it on my own strength, but I was not going to do that. I could have easily gone to my mom and said, "Mom, can I offer you life coaching for $800?" and I'm sure that she would have done that to help me achieve my goal, but achieving the goal was not what it was really about. Perhaps what it was really about was who I became in the process of achieving that goal. What characteristics did I have to step into to create income through life coaching and to learn to love myself?

Two of my girlfriends, who are also fellow life coaches, were putting on a leadership conference in Florida that I wanted to attend to support them and to grow myself. Their conference was the weekend before the second weekend when my goal had to be completed.

I had told myself that I was not allowed to go to their conference if I wasn't at 100% for my coaching goal. I wanted to punish myself if I hadn't completed my goal. I would have to suffer by staying home and not going. I was talking with my sister on the phone about this very thing and she asked me, "So, why is it that you can't go to the conference?"

As I explained to her, I realized that I was being mean to myself, I was going to choose suffering.

If I wasn't going to meet my goal, I wasn't going to meet my goal. Did it matter if I spent the weekend by myself at home or spent it at a conference meeting people? What if by going to the conference, I was able to meet a connection that would allow me to meet my goal? What if suffering was optional?

I decided to honor myself by going to the conference. Maybe I wasn't supposed to achieve the goal. Maybe that is what God wanted me to learn out of this process. What if the process was more important than the actual accomplishment of the goal? As much as my ego wanted me to try harder and do, do, do until the very last minute, I chose to be at peace, whether I met the goal or not was in God's hands.

My friend Ruby picked me up to take me to the airport. We hadn't seen one another in weeks, so drove around in circles around the airport about four times catching up. I told her how it was a week away and I hadn't met my goal and I was okay with it.

Ruby had done the photo shoot for me. Actually she and I had traded services. She offered to do a photo shoot in exchange for life coaching. It was a win-win. Initially, I had wanted that to count toward my goal, but my team said because it was a trade we didn't exchange money, that it didn't count because it wasn't actually income.

As we started on our 3rd loop around the airport, I asked her, "How much would you have charged me for the photo shoot?"

She calculated it in her head, "With taxes and everything, probably $967.71."

It was then that I had an epiphany. I got out my checkbook; "Here is a check for $967.71. I will send you an invoice for your life coaching."

I had achieved my goal. It was that easy and it was that hard. What if I had chosen not to honor myself by going to the leadership conference in Florida? I might never have achieved my goal. That answer had been in front of me for the past seven weeks. It was so close to me the whole time and I didn't see it.

Wow! It doesn't have to be hard.

After successfully completing both of these goals, I wrote this letter to myself:

Dear Bethany,

This is a love letter to you. For too many years I have put you last. I have been critical and judgmental of you and have expected you to be perfect. I have told you that you are not beautiful, not important, not deserving. Those were all not true.

The truth is that you are important ~ you are a princess and a daughter of the King. You were fearfully and wonderfully made in God's image. You are beautiful, inside and out. Your spirit is so positive and lively ~ it just radiates from your being-ness.

God has an incredible plan for your life and your future ~ thank you for not giving up on yourself and for not giving up on us. I love you Bethany. I choose to honor you and to show love to you. I know that you are not perfect and I love you just the way you are ~ you are imperfectly perfect!

I know that you may not believe me ~ perhaps I've been too harsh and unloving for too long. Even though you may not feel it, I love you anyway. Please forgive me for not being loving to you in the past. Please forgive me for treating you poorly and saying things that did not build you up.

I know that you desire to be loved and cherished more than anything else. I now realize that it starts with me. I love you and I cherish you. I choose to love you fully, completely, and unconditionally. Through God's strength I choose to love you as He loves you.

I choose to honor you with my words, thoughts, and actions. I choose to spend quality time with you and do things that you enjoy ~ laying in the pool reading a book, sitting outside, hiking, biking, running, walking, scrapbooking, card making, barbecuing, picnicking, watching a movie together, reading a book together, praying together, just being present with you. I love you today and always and promise to always shower you and honor you with self-love.

I choose to put God first and allow Him to be the center of our relationship. I am so sorry for trying to do everything on my own strength. I now realize that was foolishness. I am human and I will always fail and disappoint. That is why I choose to live moment by moment in God's strength ~ accepting His grace and mercy.

I know that I cannot love you completely on my own, but with God and through God I can love you completely and unconditionally, so that is what I choose to do. I am learning that only when I love you (me) completely, can I be loved by someone else completely. I love you, Bethany, fully and completely.

Love, ~ Me

For too long I had been my own worst enemy. I had spoken words of condemnation and judgment on myself. I had held myself to the impossible standard of perfection, refusing to acknowledge my humanity. This was driven by ego, the need to look good, the need to be perfect, the need to be right. Those programs have not served me. In fact, they've held me back from living out my greatness and from sharing the greatness of who I am with the world.

I choose to let go of the life I had planned, so as to have the life that is waiting for me! I choose to live out of my heart, not my head, following the Holy Spirit's lead. I choose to act "as if," by stepping into characteristics that I AM (even when I don't feel like I am) and let the feelings catch up. I choose to be free! Free to be me and to share the gift of myself with the world!

PART III

Love Never Fails

CHAPTER 20:

The Truth About Love

God is Love.[21]
God is patient.
God is kind.
God does not envy.
God does not boast.
God is not proud.
God does not dishonor others.
God is not self-seeking.
God is not easily angered.
God does not keep records of wrongs.
God does not delight in evil, but rejoices with the truth.
God always protects.
God always trusts.
God always hopes.
God always perseveres.
God NEVER fails![22]

People will fail me. People will disappoint me. God will never disappoint me. Never!

What if I could trust Him totally and completely with my life? What if God loves me the way that I've always desired to be loved? What if God pursues me? What if He cherishes me? How amazing would it feel to be loved that fully and that completely? What if God would never give me a broken heart? What if he takes all the pieces of my broken heart and puts them back together, using unbreakable superglue that creates a masterpiece!?!

"For the LORD your God is living among you. He is a mighty savior. He will take delight in you with gladness. With his love, he will calm all your fears. He will rejoice over you with joyful songs." ~ Zephaniah 3:17 NLT

What if God loves me with a perfect love?

"There is no fear in love. But perfect love drives out fear, because fear has to do with punishment. The one who fears is not made perfect in love." ~ 1 John 4:18 NIV

What if I could live life without fear? How would that feel? What if fear is of the devil? That would mean that anything that involves fear is not of God. How many times in the Bible does God tell me not to fear? He doesn't want me to live in fear. He wants me to live in freedom! If I choose to embrace God's perfect love, I can live without fear and in perfect peace.

How amazing would that feel — to never have to fear again?

What if I didn't have to fear not being loved and growing old alone? What if I didn't have to fear being hurt again? What if I didn't have to fear bad things that might happen? That doesn't mean that they won't happen. What it does mean is that I can trust God through the process and know that He is right there with me.

"I have told you all this so that you may have peace in me. Here on earth you will have many trials and sorrows. But take heart, because I have overcome the world." ~ John 16:33 NLT

What if fear is nothing but an illusion? What if fear is **F**alse **E**vidence **A**ppearing **R**eal? What if running toward fear, instead of running away from it, causes the mirage of fear to disappear? I don't know how many times in my life I have held myself back and played it safe because I was afraid.

Let's look closely at the situation with my ex-boyfriend...

What was I afraid of? That since He was "the one," I would end up being alone.

And what was I afraid of if I was alone? That no one would love me.

And what if no one loved me? Then that would prove that I'm not worthy of love.

When I really drilled down what my fear was, I found I was afraid that I was not worthy of love. But was that the truth? No. The truth is, I AM worthy of love. The truth is that I am God's masterpiece. The truth is that I was fearfully and wonderfully made. The truth is that God loved me so much that He sent his son to die for me. God's Word is the Truth and it does not lie. God loves me. He will never leave me or forsake me. I am never alone.

There is an old Indian Legend that talks about the battle between love and fear:

> An elder was teaching his grandchildren about life. He said to them, "A fight is going on inside me, it is a terrible fight and it is between two wolves. One wolf is evil — he is fear, anger, envy, sorrow, regret, greed, arrogance, self-pity, guilt, resentment, inferiority, lies, false pride, competition, superiority, and ego. The other is good — he is joy, peace, love, hope, sharing, serenity, humility, kindness, benevolence, friendship, empathy, generosity, truth, compassion, and faith. This same fight is going on inside you, and inside every other person, too." They thought about it for a minute and then one child asked his grandfather, "Which wolf will win?" The old man simply replied, "The one you feed." ~ Paul Keeps Horse[23]

What if I do have "two wolves" inside of me? What if one is my "flesh" that is based out of fear? What if that is my natural tendency as a human to live in fear? What if the other wolf is the Holy Spirit and God's perfect love? What if the one who wins is the one that I feed? What if the more I feed my fears, worries, and doubts, the more I give strength to that wolf? What if the more I focus on the Truth of God's Word and speak that over my life, the more inner strength I have to live a life of love?

For so much of my life I lived in fear. I didn't know that there was another option. My mind was filled with worries, regrets, judgments, doubts, scarcity, and lack. I thought that was just the way life was. That was reality. What if that doesn't have to be my reality? What if I can choose my reality?

If I had a choice, would that be the reality I want? Heck no! Why would I choose to live a life of fear over a life of freedom? That's just craziness! Yet, that is what I had done my whole life. And now that I am aware of the choice, I can choose my new reality.

So, how do I feed the wolf of love? The answer lies in this verse:

"Teacher, which one is the greatest of the Laws?" Jesus said to him, "'you must love the Lord your God with all your heart and with all your soul and with all your mind.' This is the first and greatest of the Laws. The second is like it, 'You must love your neighbor as you love yourself.' ~ Matthew 22:36-39 NLT

What if the way to ensure I am feeding the wolf of love is to love God and to love people?[24] What if by me accepting God's love and allowing Him to fill me with His love, I can then love others with His perfect love out of my overflow? What if I don't have to do it on my own strength? What if once I am emptied of my ego and myself, I can be filled to overflowing with His perfect love? What if it's not even really me, but rather Him working through me?

All my life I would give and give to others and in doing so deplete myself. What if it didn't have to be that way? What if I allowed God to be the source of my love instead of trying to love on my own strength? What if I could allow myself to get filled to overflowing with His love? What if that allowed me to give out of my abundance instead of draining me? What if I allowed God's love to fill me to overflowing so that everyone I came into contact with could not help but get splashed with His living water and perfect love?

What if true love is more about giving love than receiving love? I always thought that I had something missing inside — a void that needed to be filled. I sought out to have that void filled by someone else and was always disappointed.

What if that void was meant to be filled by God? What if no one and nothing else could satisfy that void except for Him, the creator of the Universe? What if by allowing Him to fill me with His perfect love, I am complete, not lacking anything? What if once I allow myself to be loved completely by Him, I have the capacity to truly love another person, the way that He loves me?

CHAPTER 21:

I Am Cherished

One Friday evening, I had a date night with God. Together we watched *The Passion of Christ*. I had not yet seen this movie. I remember it coming out while I was deployed to Kosovo and I had not yet created the opportunity to watch it. So, God and I watched it together.

Not long ago, God shared a picture with me which really spoke to my spirit. It was a picture of Jesus hugging a little girl. Whenever I look at this picture, I feel such peace and comfort, as though God is hugging me. I have this picture on my laptop and on my phone as screen savers. I often look at it whenever I need a God hug or need to be reminded that He is right here with me.

As I watched the movie, *The Passion of Christ*,[25] there were points in the movie where my heart just ached with sadness at what was being done. It was at these points, that I held my phone in my hand, looked down at this picture, and allowed myself to be comforted and embraced by God. He would speak to my spirit and say, "It's okay Bethany. You already know the end of the story." I took comfort in His embrace and in knowing that what I was seeing was not how the story ends.

Just as He had comforted me in that moment, He has comforted me throughout my journey. There have been times when I felt I just could not go on — that I could not handle any more. During those times, God gently spoke into my spirit, "My darling, keep your eyes on me, not your circumstances. This is not how the story ends."

That has been such a source of comfort and strength for me. Comfort in knowing that what I was feeling was going to come to an end and strength in knowing that He has me in the palm of His hand and has an AMAZING future planned just for me!

"For I know the plans I have for you," declares the LORD, "plans to prosper you and not to harm you, plans to give you hope and a future." ~ Jeremiah 29:11 NIV

The Passion of Christ — His passion is for *me*. He went through all that suffering, all that pain and torment for *me* — because He loves *me*. In fact, he cherishes *me*! Yes, *me*! If I was the only person here on this earth, Jesus still would have suffered and died for *me*, so that I could live forever with Him. He loves *me* that much. He loves *me* soooo much! More than I can even comprehend! He loves me fully and completely in the way that I've always wanted to be loved. He loves me passionately and jealously! He would do anything for me. He loves me!!!

And I know this in my head. It even gives me peace within, but I haven't always fully embraced it in my heart. I had a God-sized void in my heart, which I had been trying to fill with people, things, and accomplishments. It was an insatiable void that was never satisfied and always ended up with disappointment. My whole life I had been hoping, praying, and searching for "Mr. Right." Over and over I would be disappointed. When I finally met someone who I thought was "the one" — someone who I thought completed me — I was then dashed with disappointment yet one more time.

What if no one could complete me except my creator Himself? What if He created me that way — with a God-sized void? What if this God-sized void could only be filled by God Himself? What if He created me that way, so that I would finally find myself in Him?

What if He gave me freedom of choice; free will to live my life as I wanted? What if He had a perfect plan and a perfect design for my life that was tailor-made just for me? What if all I had to do was to step into that plan — into who He created me to be? And, if I chose less than that, He would let me because He loves me, but what He really wants for me more than anything else is His *very best*!

What if the only way to truly know that plan was to experience it as I was walking it out? What if God just gives me bits and pieces of the incredible plan that He has for my life, so I won't run ahead of Him, mess things up, and do things on my own strength? What if He gives me bits and pieces of His plan, just to wet my whistle — just so I know that there are good things ahead? What if he only gives me enough light for the step that I'm on, so that I can trust Him moment by moment, step by step, day by day?

What if I, being made in God's image, have all the characteristics of God himself within me? What if God gave me talents, interests, passions, and personality traits that were uniquely made just for me to fulfill a unique God-ordained purpose? What if He had placed a Bethany-specific greatness inside of me that all I had to do was step into?

Wow! That's some pretty big possibility! How exciting and how liberating!

So, to walk in the freedom of God's perfect plan, all I have to do is give it over to Him and let Him take care of everything? I don't have to worry? I don't have to stress? I don't have to have it all figured out? All I have to do is trust in Him, be obedient to His Word and His calling on my life — trust Him fully and completely with every area of my life? It sounds too good to be true. What's the catch? There has to be a catch.

Well, there is. I have to die to myself. I'm not talking my physical self, but my "flesh," my fleshly spirit, my human nature. God is into relationships. What He wants is to be in a relationship with each and every one of us, including me. When I chose to be in relationship with God and asked Him to lead my life instead of me leading it, He gave me a gift- the gift of Holy Spirit. The Holy Spirit is a guide, who speaks to me in a still small voice and guides my way.

> *"So I say, let the Holy Spirit guide your lives. Then you won't be doing what your sinful nature craves. The sinful*

nature wants to do evil, which is just the opposite of what the Spirit wants. And the Spirit gives us desires that are the opposite of what the sinful nature desires. These two forces are constantly fighting each other, so you are not free to carry out your good intentions. But when you are directed by the Spirit, you are not under obligation to the law of Moses.

When you follow the desires of your sinful nature, the results are very clear: sexual immorality, impurity, lustful pleasures, idolatry, sorcery, hostility, quarreling, jealousy, outbursts of anger, selfish ambition, dissension, division, envy, drunkenness, wild parties, and other sins like these. Let me tell you again, as I have before, that anyone living that sort of life will not inherit the Kingdom of God.

But the Holy Spirit produces this kind of fruit in our lives: love, joy, peace, patience, kindness, goodness, faithfulness, gentleness, and self-control. There is no law against these things!" ~ Galatians 5:16-23 NLT

CHAPTER 22:

The Value of Wasted Time

"Sometimes the best answer to a prayer is the silence of God asking us to wait."
~ Trena Reed

I remember leaving the weekend seminar that I had attended in Waikiki, with a burning question in my mind, "What is the value of wasted time?" I hated wasted time. I felt as though my ex-husband had wasted years of my life — while we were dating and during the two short years that we were married. After our divorce, I vowed not to have my time wasted ever again!

This vow translated to every area in my life. I was all about efficiency, whether it was how I ran errands or how I did things around the house, efficiency was the bottom line. I would not arrive anywhere early, but always right on time. I didn't like sitting around and wasting my time by arriving somewhere early. At work, I would stay at my computer, accomplishing as much as I could before going to any meetings. Most meetings started late anyways and it was not an efficient use of my time to get to a meeting early.

I did not like to waste my time and I did not like interacting with people who would waste my time. As far as I was concerned, dating was a waste of time. My party line was, "I am content being single and don't like to waste my time, however I am willing to share my life with someone if the right person comes along."

When I first started dating my ex-boyfriend, I shared with him my philosophy on wasted time and I told him, "I'm willing to waste my time on you." How romantic is that? That was my way of protecting myself — of keeping up my wall of protection. It kept me from getting hurt. It kept me "safe."

God allowed me to reach a state of brokenness and stay there, so I could learn the value of wasted time. My default was to hurry up and get better and not waste my time being sad. I wanted to just suck it up and move on. But this time, I didn't want to put back up the wall of protection. I didn't want to pretend that the feelings weren't there. I took a risk and opened myself up to love again and I was sad that it didn't work out.

For many years, I did not allow myself to feel. Instead, I pretended I was tough, that it didn't matter and that I was fine. I didn't want to be numb and calloused anymore. I wanted to do things differently this time. This time I chose to give my feelings to God, to trust Him with the process and to trust His timing.

Waiting on God and trusting the process took a lot longer than I would have chosen. There were days that I just wanted to be done with the waiting, and yet, what was I going to do — go back to doing things on my own strength? No, that wasn't an option. I guess I just had to keep waiting it out — trusting God and His perfect timing.

"God is never in a hurry. He never rushes a sunrise, never skips through a season. He doesn't grow a sapling into a mighty tree overnight, nor speed up the development of a baby in a mother's womb.

God refuses to cut any corners with me. He doesn't just one day insert His character into my life, but rather molds and shapes it at His will. There are many things I wish God would get on with in my life. Promises He has given me that have yet to be fulfilled, hopes and dreams of mine yet to be realized.

I get the sense that with my life, He is writing a story; yet when I flip to the end, all I see are blank pages. God never allows my impatience to speed-up His plan. His plan for my life doesn't unfold in large chunks, but rather one-day-at-a-time, in fact, one-moment-at-a-time.

The intimacy with my Lord comes through the process and not so much the outcome. I've discovered far more about God and His character through the journeying as opposed to the arriving."[26] ~ David Stephens

What if it was through the waiting that God was developing my character to make it more like His? What if He was actually strengthening me through the waiting process? What if in my weakness, He was strong? What if the strength that He was developing in me was an inner strength — a strength of spirit? What if it did not rely on my human strength, but rather His strength through me?

> *"But those who wait on the Lord*
> *Shall renew their strength;*
> *They shall mount up with wings like eagles,*
> *They shall run and not be weary,*
> *They shall walk and not faint."* ~ Isaiah 40:31 NASB

What if true wasted time is time spent mourning the past or worrying about the future? What if the only way to not waste time is to be fully present in each and every moment? What if the only time that I personally have control over is the present moment? What if in each and every moment I have choice? What if I can determine how I choose to feel, how I choose to react, and what I choose to do? What if there is absolutely nothing that I can do to change the past or to change other people's choices?

What if by re-playing the past in my mind, I end up stuck and not experiencing the present moment? What if the best way for me to affect my future is through the choices that I make now, in this present moment? I have heard it said that "worrying is like a rocking chair, it gives you something to do, but doesn't get you anywhere." What if that's true?

*"That is why I tell you not to worry about everyday life —
whether you have enough food and drink, or enough
clothes to wear. Isn't life more than food, and your body
more than clothing? Look at the birds. They don't plant or
harvest or store food in barns, for your heavenly Father
feeds them. And aren't you far more valuable to him than
they are? Can all your worries add a single moment to
your life?*

*"And why worry about your clothing? Look at the lilies of
the field and how they grow. They don't work or make their
clothing, yet Solomon in all his glory was not dressed as
beautifully as they are. And if God cares so wonderfully
for wildflowers that are here today and thrown into the fire
tomorrow, he will certainly care for you. Why do you have
so little faith?*

*"So don't worry about these things, saying, 'What will we
eat? What will we drink? What will we wear?' These
things dominate the thoughts of unbelievers, but your heavenly Father already knows all your needs. Seek the
Kingdom of God above all else, and live righteously, and he
will give you everything you need.*

*"So don't worry about tomorrow, for tomorrow will bring
its own worries. Today's trouble is enough for today."*
~ Matthew 6:25-34 NLT

What if it were possible to live a worry free life? What if I
could trust God and His provision truly and completely?
What if I no longer chose to carry burdens that weren't
really mine to carry? What if I released all my cares to Him
and trusted him fully and completely, moment by moment,

day by day? What if living in awareness in the present moment and trusting in God is the key to living in freedom?

What if I trusted God's perfect timing? What if wasted time is actually a time of growth, healing, and preparation? What if the wasted time that I experienced in my life was actually preparing me for my next season? What if it was a stepping-stone to get me to the next level of where I'm going?

What if I had chosen to remain stuck instead of leaning into the process? I would likely still be stuck today. In fact I could have stayed stuck the rest of my life, if I hadn't been willing to do the hard work of looking inward and discovering who I really am.

As much as I would never want to go back and re-live those seasons, I wouldn't be who I am today if it wasn't for those seasons. I wouldn't have the ability to impact lives and help other people discover their inner greatness, the peace of being healed and the joy of walking in faith. What if that is the value of wasted time?

CHAPTER 23:

A Firm Foundation

"So after you have suffered a little while, He
will restore, support, and strengthen you and
he will place you on a firm foundation."
~ 1 Peter 5:10 NLT

For so many years I lived on my own strength. That worked well for me up until life started getting hard. When my strength finally failed me and I could no longer do it on my own, I hit rock bottom. It was at rock bottom where I met the eternal rock of my salvation. From rock bottom, I was able to build my life on a solid foundation — on the One who never changes.

"Therefore everyone who hears these words of mine and puts them into practice is like a wise man who built his house on the rock. The rain came down, the streams rose, and the winds blew and beat against that house; yet it did not fall, because it had its

foundation on the rock. But everyone who hears these words of mine and does not put them into practice is like a foolish man who built his house on sand. The rain came down, the streams rose, and the winds blew and beat against that house, and it fell with a great crash." ~ Matthew 7:24-27 NIV

God has given me all the answers. He has given me a new strength, a supernatural strength. God does not just want to give me strength — He wants to be my strength! I no longer have to do things on my own. I can now live in perfect freedom — in His freedom!

"But he said to me, 'My grace is sufficient for you, for my power is made perfect in weakness.' Therefore I will boast all the more gladly about my weaknesses, so that Christ's power may rest on me. That is why, for Christ's sake, I delight in weaknesses, in insults, in hardships, in persecutions, in difficulties. For when I am weak, then I am strong." ~ 2 Corinthians 12:9-10 NIV

CHAPTER 24:

Trading My Sorrow

"Joy is always present in our life, much like the sun. However, sometimes 'clouds' may mask our ability to feel it. Clouds don't make the sun go away, neither does joy ever leave you. Choose to acknowledge your joy, when it seems hidden and you will bring forth peace in all 'weather'." ~ Lisa Schilling

Just like going into the depths of depression was my choice, so was coming out of the depths of depression. I had chosen to stay stuck in the past, re-living events in my mind, and delving even further into the depths of despair.

Getting out of the pit that I had dug for myself was hard work. It was not something that I did on my own. I chose to surround myself with positive people, who would encourage me, challenge me, and who would no longer let me be stuck in my stuff. These people included my counselor, my Celebrate Recovery support group, my mastermind group, my life coaches, my friends, my family, and my primary care manager.

I intentionally chose to capture thought processes that did not serve me and replace them with the Truth of God's Word. I infused God's Truth into my life, my feelings, and my circumstances. I spoke words of encouragement to myself and surrounded myself with people who did the same. And most importantly I spent time with God — talking with Him, reading His Word, and listening to His still small voice.

Through consistent application of the above, my feelings started to shift from despair to peace. By continuously releasing everything to God, and keeping my eyes on Him, He was able to fill my mind with His perfect peace.

"You will keep in perfect peace all who trust in you, all whose thoughts are fixed on you!" ~ Isaiah 26:3 NLT

By leaning into the pain, I was able to break down, so that I could break through. The breakthrough was a journey. It was like climbing Mt. Everest and when I finally broke through and reached the top, it was then that I had peace like a river in my soul!

Although at the time, it did not feel good, I can now under-stand what James was conveying when he said,

"Dear brothers and sisters, when troubles come your way, consider it an opportunity for great joy. For you know that when your faith is tested, your endurance has a chance to grow. So let

it grow, for when your endurance is fully developed, you will be perfect and complete, needing nothing." James 1:1-4 NLT

I am nowhere near perfect. But I can say that my faith has been tested and my endurance has had a chance to grow. God has refined me in the furnace of affliction and by doing so has shaped my character to be more like that of Jesus.

It was a painful process at the time. I would not want to go back and yet I would not trade that time. It was through that experience that I was able to discover who God really was and who I really was. I was able to truly discover the love that God has for me and how He was pruning the garden of my heart.

> *"I am the true grapevine, and my Father is the gardener. He cuts off every branch of mine that doesn't produce fruit, and he prunes the branches that do bear fruit so they will produce even more. You have already been pruned and purified by the message I have given you. Remain in me, and I will remain in you. For a branch cannot produce fruit if it is severed from the vine, and you cannot be fruitful unless you remain in me.*

> *"Yes, I am the vine; you are the branches. Those who remain in me, and I in them, will produce much fruit. For apart from me you can do nothing. Anyone who does not remain in me is thrown away like a useless branch and withers. Such branches are gathered into a pile to be burned. But if you remain in me and my words remain in you, you may ask for anything you want, and it will be granted! When you produce much fruit, you are my true disciples. This brings great glory to my Father.*

"I have loved you even as the Father has loved me. Remain in my love. When you obey my commandments, you remain in my love, just as I obey my Father's commandments and remain in his love. I have told you these things so that you will be filled with my joy. Yes, your joy will overflow!" ~ John 15:1-11 NLT

God was pruning me, so that I could produce fruit for him. In John Bevere's book, *Victory in the Wilderness*, he describes the wilderness as "not the season of harvest, but of pruning and grafting."[27] That is one law of the universe that the Bible speaks to quite often, the law of sowing and reaping.

Thank God for seasons! The beautiful thing about seasons is that they are only temporary and whatever you sow is what you will reap. Thank you God for pruning me. I know that through that pruning, you were preparing me for the incredible future that you have planned for me! And, I know that harvest day is coming!

Just like when He fed the Israelites with manna each morning, He has taught me that I must rely on His strength and his sustenance daily. This is why when He taught us to pray, he said, "give us this day our daily bread."[28] God does not want me to go running off trying to do things on my own strength like I used to. Rather, He wants me to abide in Him.

God wants an intimate relationship with me. He wants me to seek him every moment of the day and to talk with Him continuously throughout the day. That is what abiding is, to be in constant companionship with the God of the Universe. Abiding is not hard. It is not doing, but being. It is resting securely in the palm of God's hand, trusting Him completely, and being in constant communication with Him.

"Always be joyful. Never stop praying. Be thankful in all circumstances, for this is God's will for you who belong to Christ Jesus."
~ 1 Thessalonians 5:16-18 NLT

What if I lived a life of gratitude —of being thankful in all circumstances? What if no matter what my circumstances, I found something to be thankful for? What if it were as simple as being alive, being able to breath, having food in my refrigerator, and gas in my car?

What if I lived with an attitude of gratitude? What if instead of taking people for granted, I felt grateful to have them in my life? What if I shared those feelings of gratitude with them on a regular basis? How would that strengthen our relationships?

What if gratitude turned what I had into enough? What if ungratefulness led to feelings of lack, jealousy, and entitlement? What if the more I focused on what I didn't have, the more disgruntled I became and the more lack I experienced? What if living in awareness and gratitude of all the blessings in my life, helped me to continuously see and experience more and more blessings?

What if each and every one of us has a choice of how we choose to experience life? What if we could choose to live a life of abundance or we could choose to live a life of scarcity? If I had a choice, I would choose abundance all the way! And so I have.

I choose to live a life of gratitude. I choose to be grateful for all the blessings that God has bestowed upon me. I choose to be grateful for what is and what is to come. I choose to be thankful for the people, things and experiences that God has allowed me be a part of. I choose to be a good steward with all that God has blessed me with, realizing that He is the source and all that I have comes from Him.

CHAPTER 25:

Living on the Edge

"Far better it is to dare mighty things, to win glorious triumphs, even though checkered by failure, than to take the rank with those poor spirits who neither enjoy nor suffer much, because they live in the gray twilight that knows neither victory nor defeat."
~ Theodore Roosevelt

For too many years I was playing small in life. I was not playing to win, but rather playing not to lose. I was playing it safe — not risking too much and conforming to what was expected of me to look good and be "successful."

For much of my life, I was sitting on the sidelines. It was safe sitting on the sidelines, it was comfortable. I didn't have to risk too much because I wasn't actually out there playing the game. I could yell out my opinion and my thoughts for how things "should" be, but I really had no skin in the game.

It's easy being an observer in life. I have nothing to risk. I can enjoy watching the game without having to do all the hard work of preparation and training. Being on the sidelines, I get to experience the joys and sadness of the game, but from a safe distance, not at the same level as the players who are in the game. Players who are out on the field experience the joy of winning and the pain of defeat in ways that those on the sidelines never get to know.[29]

Looking at my life, and me, you would never think that I was playing a small game. By the world's standards I was very successful. I excelled in everything that I did. I always got outstanding evaluations. I was "fast tracking" according to military standards.

So, why take the risk of writing this book? This is a risky book. It's vulnerable. Why "ruin" my career by airing my dirty laundry? Why don't I just wait until I retire? Play it safe. Don't make waves.

Those are the questions and recommendations that I would have told someone who was doing what I am doing, before my journey began. I understand that it might not make sense to a lot of people and I understand where they are coming from. And now that my mind has been stretched, and I have been brought into the awareness of possibility, there is no way for me to go back to playing small.

If you look back to all the great leaders in history, no one has made history by playing it safe. No one has made history by conforming to the expectations of others and playing a small game. Those who have taken risks, those who have experienced failure and chosen to get up and keep moving forward — those are people who have made a mark on history.

Will I be one of those people? Who knows, and honestly, who cares? All I know is that if I can impact the lives of those I touch, if I can help others to shift their thinking, if I can empower others to discover the greatness that is within them, then I will have lived out my purpose.

I'm choosing to live life on the edge, to take a risk, to put it all on the line. What do I have to lose, honestly? The things that I fear the most don't even exist. Fear only has as much power as I choose to give it. Fear has no power over me. It is a mirage.

I choose to run toward the mirage of fear and watch it disappear from before my eyes. I choose to live a big game. I choose to help others, through helping myself. I choose to be a role model for doing the hard work of self-discovery. It is an extremely intense process that few will undertake.

So, how about you, will you continue playing a small game or will you choose to play big and take yourself on? There is no judgment either way.

That is the cool thing about it. You can play a small game. You can go through life working to survive — just making it through. Most people do that, they are content with that and that is their choice.

Just know, if you do want to play a bigger game, you can decide at any time. There are few people who choose that road. And the few who do will willingly help you get where they have gotten if you are willing to take yourself on. You have to be serious though. You have to set the intention, keep your eyes on the goal, and keep moving forward steadfastly.

And know, when you decide to do something really big, you will encounter an equal or greater resistance to what you say you want.[30] The only way to actually accomplish what you say you want to accomplish is to keep your eye on the goal and keep moving forward, regardless of feelings, distractions, or circumstances. Your default is to prove yourself right —the little voice in your head that says, "You can't do this."

Keep your eye on the goal, don't listen to the naysayers, don't be distracted by your circumstances, and keep moving forward.

Surround yourself with people who will encourage you, challenge you, and build you up. Seek out those who are at a higher level than you, who are currently where you want to be. You may have to shift who is in your inner circle, so that you will not be pulled back into your comfort zone and a life of mediocrity.

Everything that you really want in life — all the good stuff is outside of your comfort zone. When you get comfortable with being uncomfortable, when you live outside of your comfort zone — this is when you will start living the life of your dreams!

Right after taking the picture above, I sat down and journaled the following,

> I've been waiting two years for this. I let it go! This is it and I'm satisfied. I am satisfied being single. I'm satisfied moving forward and growing. I'm satisfied following God's way and not my own.

> I'm letting go and letting God. I'm choosing to live life on the edge. Living out of my comfort zone all the time, pushing forward toward more, better, different — gratification (what could be). But first, I am satisfied with where I am; with all the decisions that I have made up to this point; because they have brought me to where I am today.

> God, I let go. I release everything. I release control. I choose to live my life out of control, never knowing what to expect, but always with anticipation. For I know the plans you have for me, plans for a future and a hope.[31] When I ask for bread, are you going to give

me a rock?[32] No! You're my Father! You know what's best for me. Your ways are higher than my ways. Your thoughts are higher than my thoughts.[33] What you have planned is beyond anything I could hope, dream, or imagine.[34]

You love me. You want what's best for me. You have given me my hearts desires. You have placed them within me. You have gifted me with treasures untold. Thank you God, that this is only the beginning. I am giving it all to you. It is yours. I am yours. Where you go I will follow. In this two-step of life you are my lead. Thank you that you are my partner, my life, my husband,[35] and my lead. You are all I need. You complete me.

Thank you Lord that nothing and no one will satisfy but you. If I keep chasing gratification it will always be out of my reach. But if I choose to be present in the moment, to follow your lead — I can have all the more, better, different that my heart desires and more!

God, I am complete in you. I give it to you — I have released my desire for an intimately fulfilling, fun, loving, relationship. I choose to seek that in you and you alone. If there is someone out there for me, they must go through you first, in order to find me.[36] I don't know what that looks like; I don't know what my future looks like; all I know is that it's good — real good — all my heart's desires are fulfilled.

You will restore to me the years that the swarming locust have eaten.[37] My days of mourning have come to an end.[38] My joy is in you. In you I am complete. In you I live and breathe and have my being.[39] Thank you for pursuing me. Thank you for loving me with a never-ending love.

Today I stood over the edge and let it go. I let go of what was holding me back. I let go of the past. I let go of the future. I let go of my hopes and dreams. I let go of my ex-boyfriend. I let go of expectations. I release them to you. It's all you now God. It's all you. I have died; I live in you. It wasn't even scary at all. It was exhilarating. It was freeing. I choose to walk in your freedom. The old has gone. I am a new creation.[40]

I choose to truly live out the life that you have called me to. Whatever you have planned is cool with me (remind me that I said that). I'm done with doing things my way; with being in charge; with knowing it all. You take the lead God. You know paths with twists and turns that are adventurous. I'm holding on to you while letting go. I'm all in God. Thank you!

~ Bethany

Chapter 26:

My Story, God's Glory

"If you have powerful secrets these secrets own you, if you have deep fears, these fears own you. Your children no longer are your children, but the children of those things that own you. They become children of secrets and fears. The struggle for authenticity is the struggle to become honest, trusting, and compassionate even when we have evidence not to. But this struggle creates a meaningful life and is the legacy you will leave to the next generation." ~ Patrick Dean

What if the story of my life is not actually about me? What if my story is simply a chapter in God's epic love story? What if when I was born, God handed me a pen and gave me the freedom to be the author of my life? What if my life is a storybook with blank pages and God gave me the choice of what I put on my pages? What if I have the freedom to write whatever I want to write, in whatever way I want? What if that was one of God's gifts to me — freedom of choice — of self-determination?

What if He also gave me another gift — the gift to live in true freedom? What if true freedom was giving the pen back to God and allowing Him to write my part in His story? What if God sees the big picture? What if He knows the exact purpose that I was created for and has a perfect way to allow me to live out my life purpose? What if when I give Him the pen, he creates a story that is bigger and better than anything I've ever hoped or dreamed?

What if, even when I choose to take back the pen and write on my own and mess up my story, He loves me just the same? What if when I give Him back the pen, after messing things all up, He can turn anything that I wrote into something good?

"And we know that God causes everything to work together for the good of those who love God and are called according to his purpose for them." ~ Romans 8:28 NLT

What if the purpose of my story is actually to bring God glory? What if that is why God made humans — "to rely on Him and give Him glory?"[41] What if after the whole Adam and Eve fiasco, His original plan was thwarted? What if after eating from the tree of good and evil, mankind sought to "rely on himself and seek his own glory?"[42] What if once this happened, we were separated from God? What if God is so holy and so righteous that we no longer could be in His presence once we had been exposed to evil?

What if God loved us so much that He would do anything possible to get us back, so that we could be in relationship with Him once again? What if the only way to get us back was through a sacrifice? What if God loved us so much that he gave us the ultimate sacrifice? What if the ultimate sacrifice was Him humbling himself by coming down to earth, living as we lived, and dying on the cross?[43] What if that was the only way that we might be able to live in communion with Him again?[44]

What if God is a jealous God? What if it is not the type of jealousy that we as humans know and feel, but rather a righteous jealousy? What if He is jealous for me? What if He loves me so much and wants to be in relationship with me so much that He would give His life for me? What if when I seek to live out my own selfish desires, when I am filled with vanity and focused on me, me, me — that is when He gets jealous? What if He gets jealous when I put anything else before Him?[45] And what if He loves it, when I praise Him, honor Him, worship Him, and give Him glory? What if He delights in the praises of His people?

What if God uses my tests to create my testimony? I remember God speaking this verse to me when I first started struggling through my depression:

"This sickness will not end in death. No, it is for God's glory so that God's Son may be glorified through it." ~ John 11:4 NLT

171

At that point in time, I was still in denial that I was even "sick," yet I still found this verse to be encouraging. I chose to stand on this verse, knowing that the season was not going to last forever and somehow, some way God was going to use that season of my life for His glory.

What if that's what it's really all about? What if God's fame is created when he heals and restores? And what if through the healing and restoration process, He created my testimony? What if my story is not actually about me, but about Him? What if God's purpose for bringing me to the place where I am, is for me to share what He has done in my life? What if I have been chosen to spread God's fame throughout the world through sharing my life story?

"I have appointed you for the very purpose of displaying my power in you and to spread my fame throughout the earth." ~ Romans 9:17 NLT

What if when I make my story about me, it takes away from the impact that my story could make on the world? What if by sharing my story, my story can have an impact on future generations?

"Let this be recorded for future generations, so that a people not yet born will praise the Lord." ~ Psalm 102:18 NLT

What if the fiery trials that I experienced were actually a purification process? What if they allowed me to become transparent? What if I am now a transparent vessel that allows God's light to shine through?

"Once you are purified by the fiery trials, you become transparent! A transparent vessel brings no glory to itself, but glorifies what it contains." ~ John Bevere[46]

When my life coach first talked with me about the idea of writing a book, the first thoughts that came into my head were, "You're not a writer." "Who would want to hear your story?" "No one will read it." "You're not that important."

I heard those objections, acknowledged them and chose not to believe them. I now recognized them as negative self-talk and Satan trying to discourage me.

The devil tries to do that you know. He knows what a powerful testimony my life story is, so if He can keep me discouraged and thinking that I'm not important, then he keeps me from living out my destiny and impacting lives. I am now aware of his schemes and choose not to listen to them. Instead I choose to listen to the voice of Truth.

> "But the voice of Truth tells me a different story
> And the voice of Truth says "Do not be afraid!"
> And the voice of Truth says "This is for My glory"
> Out of all the voices calling out to me
> I will choose to listen and believe the voice of Truth."
> ~ Casting Crowns

I told my life coach, "Well, I don't know what I'd even write about. If God wants me to write a book, then He'll have to tell me what to write." That evening I went to bed and woke up in the middle of the night. God gave me the title of the book, the chapter outlines, and I started writing this book that night. I knew that I had a story to tell. There are too many people out there who don't know what they don't know. There are too many people out there who believe lies and are playing a small game in life only because they do not know there is another way.

My low profile sunglasses previously would have kept me from sharing my story. "I don't want to draw attention to myself." "I'm not important." How selfish it would be for me to keep my story and all I have learned to myself. I would be keeping the gift of myself from impacting lives. And then of course, there is the shame. "I don't want people to know." "What will they think of me?" Shame hates it when we tell our story,[47] which is exactly why I am telling mine. Once I share my story with you, shame no longer has power over me.

Sharing my story with you is not shameful, it's being real and sharing the experience with others who have been or are going through the same thing. God uses everything for good. He is using all the yucky seasons in my life for good — for me to be able to support and give hope to others. It truly is a gift.

"A confession you make merely to illuminate the murky corners of your little life may end up lighting the path to freedom for a thousand other hearts." ~ Martha Beck

What if I was created for such a time as this?

"The fact is, even if you remain silent now, someone else will help and rescue the Jews, but you and your relatives will die. And who knows, you may have gained your royal position for a time like this." ~ Esther 4:14 GWT

What if when I let my own light shine it gives others permission to do the same? What if my life experiences are a gift for me to share? Satan may have tried to discourage me. He may have put obstacles in my path, but just like with Joseph, what the devil meant for harm, God intended for good.

"You intended to harm me, but God intended it all for good. He brought me to this position so I could save the lives of many people." ~ Genesis 50:20 NLT

In the movie *Secretariat*,[48] I totally identified with Penny, one of the main characters. The following characteristics struck me the most:

~ She was determined and she never gave up.
~ There were times when she doubted and was unsure, yet she continued to believe.
~ She didn't let failure and disappointment get her down.
~ She stayed humble. She did not boast. She let the results speak for themselves.
~ She did not get defensive, jealous, or intimidated.
~ She stood her ground.
~ She connected with the horse from a place of ground and center.
~ She looked beyond the circumstances into possibility.
~ She took big risks.
~ She had to give up time with her family.
~ It didn't happen overnight. It took years, consistency, determination, and planning.

- ~ She did her research and didn't go with what the experts said, but with what she knew (intuition).
- ~ She had a big vision and enrolled others in that vision.
- ~ Her motives were not carnal in nature (money, prestige), but rather loyalty to her father and his legacy and painting her dreams into reality.

I don't know how many times on this journey of self-discovery I got to the point of wanting to give up. "This is too much...I am not seeing results...Forget it." Then, I would think to myself, "So, what am I going to do — go back to playing small?" That's not even an option. Now that I am aware, now that I know what I know, there is no going back. So, I just take another step and keep moving forward.

Even though on a day-to-day basis it doesn't seem like I am seeing results, the intangible results that I have seen, felt, and experienced have been tremendous. Who I have become in this process has been astounding! I am not the same person that I was when I started this journey. Who I was then, was who I wanted to be seen as, the act I had learned to play in life to be "successful." It had worked, it had gotten me to where I was and that person was not going to get me to where I am going.

As I have intentionally pursued the path of self-discovery, God has given me a glimpse of the amazing destiny that He has planned for me. It is bigger than anything I could have ever imagined and it is not in the least bit overwhelming, because God is leading the way. In order to achieve the destiny He has planned for me, I truly have to step into the authentic greatness of who I am inside. I choose to own the greatness within me, and step into it unapologetically!

People are not going to understand why I do what I do. I am marching to the beat of a different drum — to God's drum. I have surrendered who I thought I was for who I actually am and who He designed me to be! It has been a painful process, a scary process, and a liberating process!

Just like with Penny, my family and friends might not understand. To them it may seem irresponsible and risky — sometimes it feels that way to me too; then, I re-focus my eyes on Him and He once again fills me with His strength and peace. I will keep my eyes on Him and the dreams He has placed in my heart.

I will maintain a quiet confidence, knowing who I am and knowing the end of the story. God has placed dreams in my heart and has given me promises in His Word. His promises never fail. I know the end of the story.

Just like Jesus and just like Penny, I choose to live my life in quiet confidence. I will not defend or justify, I will let my results speak for themselves. I will live with an aura of expectancy without expectations. I will stand on the promises of God's Word and trust Him and His timing fully and completely.

I will live my life and share my story, not for myself, but for His glory. I will leave a legacy through my actions, through the lives that I have touched, and through the impact that I have made on the world simply by *being* the beautiful and cherished woman of God that He designed me to be!

CHAPTER 27:

The Best Is Yet to Come!

"Entering the door of your future often requires passing through the door of your past to be healed first." ~ Os Hillman

I used to tell myself that I was not a good storyteller. The truth is, I am an incredible storyteller. I had told myself so many stories and for so long. For every single event in my life, I had made up a story around that event which gave that event meaning. The thing is that I did it unconsciously and most of the time, I told myself stories that did not serve me.

Now that I own my amazing gift of storytelling, I have a choice over what stories I choose to tell myself and the meaning that I give to events that happen in my life. Since

I am the one making up the story, I'm making up good stories that serve me well. No more playing small for me. I'm playing full out, dreaming big, and living life out loud!

I thank God that He loved me exactly where I was and the way I was and He loved me enough not to let me stay that way. This process of self-discovery, although painful and long, has been a gentle process. He has worked with me gently and met me right where I was, without judgment and without blame.

He loved me through each and every step of the journey. Once one layer of the onion was peeled back, He would gently peel back a new layer. It was always my choice whether I wanted to deal with an issue or not. I could have stayed stuck in my stuff, as I had done my whole life, and that wasn't working for me. I wanted more, better, different in my life. So, I chose to lean into the pain and lean into the process. The only way to the other side is through him and I wanted to get to the other side!

The journey of self-discovery is a lifelong process. It is a journey that will continue here on this earth until I take my last breath and will climax when I enter into eternity and fully experience who I truly am in Him.

I know that I haven't touched the surface of what God has in store for me. I may have walked in a measure of that blessing, but there is more to come! God has opportunities in my future that are going to amaze me![49] I am choosing to daily walk with an air of expectancy without expectations.

I know that God has an amazing future planned for me and I feel excited to walk the journey, following His lead, and trusting Him through the process. I will no longer limit Him by thinking that things have to look a certain way. I choose to be surprised and delighted as God reveals my future to me step-by-step, day-by-day, and moment-by-moment.

"Now all glory to God who is able to, through his mighty power at work within me, to accomplish infinitely more than I might ask or think!" ~ Ephesians 3:20 NLT[50]

Thank you God — the best is yet to come!

To be continued...

ACKNOWLEDGMENTS

A special thank you to the people and circumstances that propelled me forward on my journey of self-discovery.

Thank you to my friends, mentors and accountability partners: Ruby Muza, Kelley Togiola, Kathy Banks, Evelyn Viot, Rebekah Botello, Michelle Howe, Anna Corulli, Justin Woodhouse and Nancy Dean for providing tough love, prayers, guidance and support throughout my journey.

Thank you to my counselor, Liz Oldham and my personal life coaches who walked beside me on my journey: Kimberly Schulte, Centa Terry, Kelly Baader, Kary Oberbrunner, Tim Davis, Kirk Brandt and Julie Coppinger.

Thank you to all of the Klemmer & Associate facilitators that have spoken into my life. I am forever grateful and my heart is forever changed because of the work that you do. A special shout out to Sam Camp 23 & especially to my Heartrageous mastermind team: Paul Schultz, Russ Gunter, Cody Neff, Kim Thompson & Kirk Brandt. Thank you for loving me where I was at and loving me through the process. This book would not be a reality without your love, support and encouragement.

Thank you to all the pastors and support staff from San Antonio CityChurch. Thank you for meeting me where I was at and loving me enough not to let me stay there. Thank you for offering the hope, healing and recovery process.

Thank you to Jenny Price, Jamie Connor, Jeanne Connor, Shawn Mullin, Dan McKay and New Century Publishing for your support in reviewing and editing this book.

Thank you to my family: Mary Connor, Amy Connor, Thomas Connor Jr, Jamie Connor, Thomas Connor Sr., Lydia Connor and each of my aunts, uncles and cousins. Thank you for all the love, guidance, prayers and support that you provided as I struggled through my journey. A special thank you to my mother who is my closest confidant and friend.

And thank you to my Lord and Savior Jesus Christ. Who pursued me, guided me, gave me revelation and peace and showed me what true love really means. Thank you for never giving up on me and carrying me through my journey. Thank you for cherishing me!

END NOTES

[1] Gary Chapman. (2004). *The 5 Love Languages: How to Express Heartfelt Commitment to Your Mate.* Chicago, IL: Zondervan.

[2] John Bevere. (2001). *Under Cover: The Promise of Protection Under His Authority.* Nashville, TN: Thomas Nelson.

[3] San Antonio CityChurch, Pastor David Saathoff, February 26, 2011. www.sacitychurch.com

[4] San Antonio CityChurch, Pastor David Saathoff, February 26, 2011. www.sacitychurch.com

[5] San Antonio CityChurch, Pastor David Saathoff, February 26, 2011. www.sacitychurch.com

[6] San Antonio CityChurch, Pastor Doug Robins, October 24, 2010. www.sacitychurch.com

[7] San Antonio CityChurch, Pastor Shad Purcell, October 30, 2010. www.sacitychurch.com

[8] San Antonio CityChurch, Pastor Shad Purcell, October 30, 2010. www.sacitychurch.com

[9] San Antonio CityChurch, Pastor Shad Purcell, October 30, 2010. www.sacitychurch.com

[10] Rick Warren. *Stay Focused.* http://purposedriven.com/blogs/daily-hope/index.html?contentid=7035. (accessed July 1, 2011)

[11] www.celebraterecovery.com

[12] Leadership Performance Training. January 2011. Seminar Systems. www.seminarsystems.com

[13] "Now all glory to God, who is able, through his mighty power at work within us, to accomplish infinitely more than we might ask or think." ~ Ephesians 3:20

[14] Melody Beattie. (1992). *Codependent No More: How to Stop Controlling Others and Start Caring for Yourself.* Center City, MN: Hazelden.

[15] Melody Beattie. (1992). *Codependent No More: How to Stop Controlling Others and Start Caring for Yourself.* Center City, MN: Hazelden. pg. 41-50.

[16] Henry Cloud. John Townsend. (1992). *Boundaries: When to Say Yes How to Say No to Take Control of Your Life.* Grand Rapids: MI: Zondervan.

[17] San Antonio CityChurch Boundaries Curriculum, July 10, 2012. www.sacitychurch.com

[18] www.klemmer.com

[19] Stephen Kendrick. Alex Kendrick. (2008). *The Love Dare.* Nashville, TN: B&H Publishing Group.

[20] www.fireproofthemovie.com

[21] "God is love." ~ 1 John 4:8

[22] "Love is patient, love is kind. It does not envy, it does not boast, it is not proud. It does not dishonor others, it is not self-seeking, it is not easily angered, it keeps no record of wrongs. Love does not

delight in evil but rejoices with the truth. It always protects, always trusts, always hopes, always perseveres. Love never fails." ~ 1 Corinthians 13: 4-8

[23] http://www.twowolves.net/legend.htm, accessed Sep 23, 2012

[24] San Antonio CityChurch, Pastor Shad Purcell, July 28, 2012. www.sacitychurch.com

[25] www.thepassionofchrist.com

[26] David Stephens. My Journey. http://beliefchangers.com/blog/2011/09/17/september-17-2011-myjourney/ (accessed September 17, 2011)

[27] John Bevere. (1992). *Victory in the Wilderness: Growing Strong in Dry Times*. Apopka, FL: Messenger Press, pg. 7.

[28] Matthew 6:11 NIV

[29] Patrick Dean. Leadership Performance Training. January 2011. Seminar Systems. www.seminarsystems.com

[30] Ronnie Doss. Champion's Workshop, Corpus Christi, TX. August 30, 2012. www.klemmer.com

[31] Jeremiah 29:11 NLT

[32] Matthew 7:9 NLT

[33] Isaiah 55:8 NIV

[34] Ephesians 3:20 NLT

[35] Isaiah 54:5 NLT

[36] "A woman's heart should be so hidden in God that a man has to seek Him just to find her." ~ Max Lucado

[37] Joel 2:25 NLT

[38] Isaiah 60:20 NLT

[39] Acts 17:28 NIV

[40] 2 Cor 5:17 NIV

[41] http://www.desiringgod.org/resource-library/sermons/god-created-us-for-his-glory, (accessed October 5, 2012)

[42] http://www.desiringgod.org/resource-library/sermons/god-created-us-for-his-glory, (accessed October 5, 2012)

[43] Philippians 2:8 NLT

[44] John 3:16 NLT

[45] Exodus 20:3 NLT

[46] John Bevere. (1992). *Victory in the Wilderness: Growing Strong in Dry Times.* Apopka, FL: Messenger Press, pg. 63.

[47] Brene Brown. (2010). *The Gifts of Imperfection: Let Go of Who You Think You're Supposed to be and Embrace Who You Are.* Center City, MN: Hazelden, pg. 9.

[48] http://www.secretariat.com/

[49] "You haven't touched the surface of what God has in store for you. You may have walked in a measure of that blessing, but there's more to come. God has opportunities in your future that are going to amaze you!" ~ Joel Osteen

[50] "Now all glory to God, who is able, through his mighty power at work within us, to accomplish infinitely more than we might ask or think." ~ Ephesians 3:20 NLT

ABOUT THE AUTHOR

Bethany Connor is passionate about awakening authentic leaders. Through speaking, facilitating, & coaching she supports the transformation process of individuals and organizations in creating culture change from the inside out.

Bethany struggled through her own journey of finding her authenticity. She suffered through two years of severe depression and a life time of low self-worth and co-dependency hidden behind the mask of perfection. Through that struggle her strength was born. Now a transformed woman, her passion is to support others in their journey of self-discovery and in re-kindling the latent dreams buried deep within their hearts.

Bethany is a Lieutenant Colonel in the Army Nurse Corps and a Registered Nurse with an advanced degree as a Clinical Nurse Specialist. She also serves as a certified coach, speaker and trainer for The John Maxwell Team. She is trained as a Life Coach through Coaching Cognition. She is a graduate of Klemmer & Associates, the Premier Leadership & Character Development Company. She has been trained in Transformational Leadership and workshop facilitation through Seminar Systems. She is also a trained mentor and leader in Celebrate Recovery.

When she is not busy changing the world, you can find her running, card making or enjoying the outdoors.

Connect with Bethany:

www.bethanyconnor.com

GET YOUR WORKBOOK

Bethany L. Connor

cherished
WORKBOOK
Your Personal Journey of Self-Discovery

Cherished: One Woman's Journey to Love and Be Loved Workbook can help you to get where you've always wanted to be. Discover your authenticity by embarking on your own personal journey of self-discovery. Be prepared to have your heart transformed in the process!

Have you ever...
~ lived in a constant state of busyness?
~ been disappointed over and over again by people not meeting your expectations?
~ struggled to keep it together on the outside while falling apart on the inside?

What if you could...
~ live in a state of peace?
~ never be disappointed again?
~ be your authentic self?

Purchase your workbook at:

www.acherishedwoman.com

WORK WITH BETHANY

SPEAKER ~ FACILITATOR ~ COACH

Bethany understands the challenge of finding the right speaker. Her dynamic, passionate and authentic approach to connecting with an audience will leave your organization inspired, energized and ready to transform. Bethany not only brings light and life to listeners, but also gives them practical tools that they can apply immediately which will set them up for success both in leadership and in life. Bethany customizes the content of her materials to meet the unique needs of the population that she is serving.

Start the dialogue today to see how Bethany can support the transformation process within you, your team or your organization in creating culture change from the inside out.

Connect Bethany today to begin the conversation at:

www.bethanyconnor.com

JOIN THE MOVEMENT

Imagine a tribe of transformational leaders who are who are passionate, pro-active, self-aware mentors who cultivate and multiply a culture of empowerment and win-win. These leaders focus on relationship building and influence to achieve desired ends that are in alignment with the core values of themselves, their customers, their team members and their organizations. Character, integrity and faith are the cornerstones from which they derive their purpose. Their passion is to continuously add value to others and by doing so continually grow and refine their leadership capabilities.

Imagine a cause built around creating, nurturing and multiplying transformational leaders through development, empowerment, and contribution.

Imagine a safe and exhilarating space that allows authentic leaders to marinate new ideas, grow themselves and support one another. This spaces allows them to be refreshed and renewed so that they are able to give themselves away in the development and multiplication of the next generation of transformational leaders.

Find out more and get your FREE copy of The Authentic Leader's Manifesto at:

www.bethanyconnor.com

Transforming the way you Lead, Love & Live!